License To Parent

License To Parent

On Becoming a Professional Parent

Kaela Austin, M.A.
Cydney Kirschbaum, M.A.

Word Association Publishers
205 Fifth Avenue
Tarentum, Pennsylvania 15084

NOTE

In this book, we avoid the awkward locutions he/she, him/her. We generally use the more traditional male pronouns which present less stylistic difficulty. The reader should understand that "she" could be substituted for "he" in most instances when it is used in this text to refer to a non-gender noun such as 'child'. The same is true of "he" substituting for "she" whenever the latter is used in the same context.

The authors have also chosen to use the first person to avoid confusion.

Book Design: Katja Elk
...and to Sheila Kutner, my Damon, thanks for everything, Pythias

Printed in the United States of America.

ISBN: 1-932205-19-5
Library of Congress Control Number: 2003116742

Word Association Publishers
205 Fifth Avenue,
Tarentum, Pennsylvania 15084
www.wordassociation.com

Dedication

This book is dedicated to our grandparents who came to this country in their youth for a chance at a new and better life. They dared to come as teenagers. They could not even speak the language. They wanted to give their unborn children and their children's children a chance to live with freedom, honor, and human dignity.

We dedicate this book to all of those parents and grandparents who came to this country in search of a better life for their families. They speak on behalf of everyone - all cultures - all religions - all ethnicities.

We thank you.

TABLE OF CONTENTS

Kaela's story

~~~~~~

It was 1967. I was 28-years-old. My baby girl was laid in my arms for the first time. I counted her fingers. I counted her toes. I marveled at the miracle of her birth. The song that came to mind was from "The King and I" and I had to sing,"Getting to know you, getting to know all about you, getting to like you, getting to hope you like me..."

We left the hospital. I found myself all alone with my daughter. Frightened and anxious I trembled at the thought of the responsibility of being a mother. In the depths of my soul in the deepest part of myself I was terrified! I didn't know what I was supposed to do. I didn't know how I was supposed to do it. On the inside I was silently crying for help. On the outside I tried to look confident. Did everybody know something I didn't know?

Early one morning later that year, Dr. Haim Ginott's face and voice blasted through my small apartment. He was on television. I stopped everything I was doing and sat glued to his every word. His wisdom about listening and valuing children to help them become themselves in the world was a transforming experience. I felt so fortunate. My secret internal cry for help had been answered.

I attended one of his seminars and began to study the techniques and systems that mapped out the way for me to grow my child into the person I hoped she would become some day.

In 1969 a wonderful baby boy was born to our family. His name was Lucas Austin. In 1971, through a series of horrible and incomprehensible circumstances, Lucas was rushed to the hospital in convulsions. After a week-long vigil at his bedside, Lucas died.

Four-year-old Cydney needed to find a way to survive the loss of her brother and I needed to find a way to survive the loss of my son.

We grieved together and moved to Los Angeles in April 1971, trying to make a new life for ourselves. We looked for answers together.

Our education, our experiences, and our life together merged to guide us to create a new paradigm for learning. Our parenting classes, A License to Parent, led to this book which we offer to everyone who wants to be a strong supportive parent, to create the space for children to manifest their unique selves in a society that expects uniformity.

The work is designed to teach parents and children how to talk to each other, how to listen to each other, and how to be curious about each other's position in the world. We want to learn about children: What are they thinking? What do they hear us say? How do they process our needs for them and for ourselves?

In this book you will discover and validate the parenting skills you already have that are working for you and your family. You will learn new tools to communicate, and you will learn how to support your children to become their best selves. We hope you will read and communicate, laugh and learn, and use this book to become successful, professional parents.

Cydney's story

~~~~~~

I had just turned four. Suddenly my world exploded. My parents separated. My father stayed in Philadelphia. My mother and I moved to Los Angeles. I could remember that there had been four of us. Now there were only two. When I was 3 years old I remember being so happy with having a brother and loving him so very much. I remember caring for Lucas so deeply that when he entered a room I knocked him over with my hugs.

At seven I knew my mother was different. Her words, actions and behaviors were not like the other parents. I felt valued, cared about, listened to, and included in our lives. My mother spoke to me with respect and consideration. That doesn't mean we didn't disagree or argue. It doesn't mean I was the perfect kid either.

When I was nine years old I began to see and understand how my mom was talking and listening. I consciously chose to imitate certain behaviors she was modeling. I loved spending time with her.

As I grew into my teens and young adulthood, I realized that the style of communication I had been learning and experiencing provided me with many advantages. After college and being in New York for several years in a job that I found to be meaningless and insignificant, I came to Los Angeles. I became a certified Parent Effectiveness Trainer.

After being trained and presenting dozens of parenting classes I decided to go back to school for a degree in psychology. I hold two masters degrees, one in Marriage and Family Therapy and a second in Clinical Psychology.

I now have a family of my own. My husband and I are talking and listening to our two sons with respect and consideration. We can see, hear and feel the positive, valuable effects of these communication skills and techniques. And we are teaching our children the most important lesson that my mom taught me: to trust yourself and to trust your intuition.

Thanks Mom.

~~~~~~

> Parent Application Form
> Self-Test for Parents and
> Potential Parents

What is your parenting style? Submissive? Controlling? Coaching? Teaching?

(Circle one)

1) Your child comes home with two different art projects.

Do you say...

    a) What a fabulous artist you are!

    b) You're great!

    c) I see lines and colors

    d) Only two? Where's more?

2) It's morning, your eight-year-old says, "I'm not going to school today."

Do you say...

    a) So, you don't want to go to school.

    b) Everybody goes to school. Get dressed now!

    c) If you went to bed on time you wouldn't be so tired.

    d) Stay home. It's your life.

3) Your teenager is going to a party Friday night.

Do you say...

    a) Are there going to be any parents there?

    b) Are there going to be drugs and alcohol?

c) Curfew is 11:00 pm. Be on time.

d) I'd like to hear more about what's going on.

4) Your 18-month-old is biting, hitting, and shoving.

Do you...

a) Leave the area when he starts this behavior.

b) Say, "No hitting."

c) Bite him back to show him how it feels.

d) Remove him from the problem and whisper, "People are not for biting."

5) Your 15-year-old misses the school bus.

Do you...

a) Drive him to school feeling angry and resentful.

b) Tell him it's his problem.

c) Yell at him, and tell him he's irresponsible.

d) Talk to come up with solutions.

6) Your two-year-old is throwing a screaming tantrum in the supermarket.

Do you...

a) Buy him a candy bar to keep him quiet.

b) Yank his arm and tell him to be quiet.

c) Tell him you can't hear what he is saying in his upset voice.

d) Leave the store embarrassed with a screaming child.

7) Does your three-year-old listen to you because

a) You listen to him.

b) He's frightened.

c) You're angry.

d) He's good.

8) Your two-and-a-half-year-old wants to turn on the TV before breakfast.

Do you...

a) Click it off.

b) Give a scowl.

c) Smile and take away the remote.

d) Talk about his feelings.

Apply for your Professional Parent™ license at the end of the workbook.

The license will certify the bearer as a Professional Parent™.

Record your answers to the questions above. We'll compare them to your answers at the end of the book.

Parenting ABC's

Acceptance, Belief, Communication

INTRODUCTION

~~~~~~

We can imagine what you're thinking. Here are more experts trying to tell me how to raise my children. Maybe you've already been a parent for over 20 years. You may even have grandchildren. Who are we to tell you what to do?

Cydney and I are both parents. I am a grandparent, too. Cydney is a daughter, wife, and mother of two wonderful and challenging boys. Since starting my Marriage, Family and Child counseling practice over 25 years ago, I've helped thousands of families find answers to their child-rearing questions. Since 1992 Cydney and I have been teaching classes and workshops together. When parents begin to explore and question the problems within their family structure, they often discover problems within themselves. Such problems can include frustration with having to repeat requests to their children, tantrums, control issues, managing feelings and problem solving.

Parents often hear the words of their own parents coming out of their mouths. When you were a kid, after a parent said something particularly harmful to you, didn't you say to yourself, "I'm never going to talk to my children like that." And here you are today, doing exactly what you swore you'd never do. How does that happen?

The goal of this book is:

- **To teach parents to communicate more effectively and responsibly.**
- **To confront unacceptable behavior.**
- **To set limits.**
- **To express approval appropriately.**
- **And to have fun.**

And speaking of having fun…

We would like to introduce you to our pig family: The Pickles. Let us explain. Do you recall the story of the "Three Little Pigs"? Just like you, each little pig wanted to become a separate, unique individual. Just like you they wanted to be good communicators with a strong family structure. The first little pig's house of straw didn't work. The second little pig's house of sticks didn't work. What was wrong? They didn't have enough information.

So together, the three little pigs gathered all manner of bricks and the best collection of state-of-the-art tools to fashion a structure that would work – that would keep them safe physically and emotionally.

Problem-solving can be scary. But with the right instruction manual and the best tools, we can all create and be part of a happy, strong family with communication skills as the solid foundation. We will use the pig family, The Pickles, to bring relevance, humor and levity to parenting.

By consciously choosing to become a more effective parent you are doing something meaningful. This book will be your road map to reaching that goal. You will discover new ways to communicate effectively. We will show you, and teach you, and give you the experience of positive parenting. You can build a family based on communication and respect. It can be your legacy.

Soon you will be speaking and listening differently and enjoying the benefits of more effective relationships with everyone who matters to you—your children, your partner, your friends, yourself, and the people you work with. You are embarking on a transformation. What you learn you can pass on to everyone around you. They will want to learn it too, because it works.

Wouldn't it be wonderful if the job of "parent" had a real job description, set of rules, or instructions delivered to you when you were presented with your child for the first time? Well, neither Cydney nor I got handed that job description. We never received the instruction book. So we wrote it. It includes the parenting job description we always wanted for ourselves. We believe....

- **The job of the parent is to teach children how to identify and express their needs and feelings.** *Wow!*

- **Children need an adult to take them seriously and help them behave appropriately in order to develop as self-actualized human beings.** *Wow!*

- **The job of the child is to live, laugh, love, and learn.** *Cool!*

Isn't it odd that one needs a license to drive, to drink, to fish, yet we don't need a license to raise a child? Having a child may be natural, but parenting requires some work, a little practice, gobs of patience, and a sense of humor. Completing this coursework and using what you learn will earn you your "License to Parent." Let's get started!

Cydney and I are offering our best counsel based on our personal experience and the latest research about successful parenting. We are talking about the kind of parenting that produces a self-actualized, successful person who can navigate in the world. We'll take a look at ways to resolve the critical issues that arise in families.

Some of the strongest and deepest issues between parent and child are drugs, sibling rivalry, managing anger, hurt feelings, and how to discipline. The issues go on and on. We will help you understand what has happened to bring you to the problems you are experiencing, what to do to alter that experience, and how to have the most effective communication between you and your child – no matter what their age.

Being a parent and facing these issues is a little bit like peeling an onion. There are many, many layers to deal with and sometimes we're going to cry...a lot! So, we'll add a pinch of patience, a dash of humor, a cup of communication, a lot of love and we have the fixings for a delicious, satisfying family stew — a delicious, rewarding relationship with our family members.

Raising the Kids or Raising the Roof

The new generation of parents is beginning to see parenting as a set of skills that can be learned. They are not buying the myth that child rearing is natural. **Childbirth** is natural—**child rearing** is not! The belief that parenting is easy is ridiculous. How are we supposed to know how to do something when we have absolutely no experience?

Some of your peers may have been raised with the philosophy that "children should be seen and not heard". When you were a youngster it was not okay to have opinions that were different from those of your parents. And to express those opinions was unthinkable! Self-expression was a sure sign of disrespect, punishable by spanking, getting yelled at, or a one-way ticket to your room.

If you are a controlling parent, you may be taken aback when your child questions one of your decisions. You may use the old "Because I said so" approach or even banish him to his room if he persists. What is really going on here? Putting the child "in his place" might temporarily satisfy your need for peace, but ultimately the two of you will pay the price of this inadequate communication style. Your refusal to hear him out teaches him to withhold his true feelings. Therefore he learns to identify you as the person who keeps him from expressing those feelings.

Your Family Identity

~~~~~~

We were all influenced by television, films, and literature as children. If you are from "The Brady Bunch" generation, then that is the family construct that is your reality. Maybe you grew up with "Father Knows Best" or "The Cosbys" or "The Simpsons". Which television show or movie skews the view of reality in your mind? From these sources you have internalized your prevailing view of the world. What we want you to know is that you are not your concepts, beliefs or ideas. These were all given to you by your parents, authority figures, and/or idols. They in turn had their concepts, ideas, and beliefs given to them by their parents, authority figures and idols.

In addition to being influenced by the media, your personality tends to develop into that of your mother and/or your father, the opposite of your mother or father, or a combination of both of these. What we want you to understand is that these constructs are all **learned** behaviors. That's the bad news.

Here's the good news. We can change a behavior by becoming aware of it, having the courage to identify it, and practicing the skills to alter it.

A word about opposites: As a child, if you were controlled and punished, a decision you might make as an adult is to never control or punish your own child. If, as a child, you were permitted excessive freedom and no restrictions, a decision you might make is to be in control of your child and impose tight rules and regulations. Either way you are not attending to the child in front of you and his particular needs.

The opposite of love is not hate. The opposite of LOVE is INDIFFERENCE. Love is a strong emotion, and indifference is the absence of emotion.

This workbook is designed to help you identify your family constructs: the opinions and behaviors that were given to you. It is important for you to see which ones you want to keep, because they work for you and enhance your life; it is also important to identify which constructs you want to discard, because they are harmful to your relationships.

Your Inner Voice

What we believe about ourselves is called our "inner voice". This inner voice is the internalized voice of the mother, the father, the teacher, the coach, the clergy and/or other authority figures. You can identify it because many times it is critical. We believe what our negative inner voice says about us. It might sound like this: "You're stupid. You'll never look good enough. You're too fat. You're too thin. You don't deserve it. You'll never have enough. You're a slob. You'll never amount to anything. You're a loser." Unfortunately, we believe what our inner voice says.

Ouch!

The inner voice, by constantly commenting negatively on our character, misshapes the personality by giving a false, limiting, critical sense of self. It impairs the integrity of the child and limits life's possibilities. Raised with criticism, a child will grow up to feel insecure and not trust himself and his decisions. He may be afraid to make a commitment and therefore be passive and look to others for approval. He may imitate his parents and learn to be critical of himself and others.

AHHH!

7

When we are raised to satisfy the expectations of our parents and care-givers, we look outside ourselves to feel "okay". So when your child comes downstairs and is wearing a red dress, blue socks, green shoes and a yellow belt and you say, "You look like a Christmas tree. The yellow belt doesn't match anything. Are you color blind or something?" The child will be sad, unsure and think negatively, "I'm not all right. I can't do this dressing thing." The child will then follow you back upstairs for you to help her change into blue and pink. From then on your child might always question if she has done it "right"- right according to you. Or your child might get angry and stuff down the emotion. That's how we create the need for outside approval. Do you want to do this to your child?

Let's try to get a different perspective. The child comes downstairs wearing a red dress, blue socks, green shoes, and a yellow belt. You say, "I see a little girl wearing a red dress, blue socks, green shoes, and a yellow belt!" She says, "Yes! I wanted to look like a rainbow today!" Your child feels accepted, respected and thinks, "I did it! I'm okay. I'm wonderful."

It is not only the *negative* inner voice of our parents that we internalize. If a child is raised by parents who respect him, treat him with honor and dignity, his inner voice may sound like this: "I'm worthwhile. I'm important. I have value." The child can trust himself. The decisions we make about ourselves between Wow! the ages of one and eight can last a lifetime.

Inner Voice and Persona

Our public persona is our "act" – what we present for others to see. The persona may be a display of kindness, compassion, integrity, or respect...masking our feelings of distrust, self-protection, insecurity, or defensiveness. In our act, we may think one thing and do another.

Here is an example of thinking one thing and doing another:

Your two-year-old is crying for candy in the supermarket. You say, "No, we'll have some after dinner." The child throws a fit. You feel like a bad parent. In order to make the child stop crying and still be perceived by others as a good parent, you give him a small piece of candy. He stops crying. You put a smile on your face, but you really feel frustrated, manipulated and angry.

Hmmm!

Then there is our "true self", which is neither the internalized mother, father, or the opposite of them. It is also *not* our public persona. The true self is the part that remains when the critical inner voice is stilled. It is that part of us that makes its own decisions. It is the part of us that has the ability to distinguish good from evil, right from wrong, loyalty from disloyalty. If we raise our children to be individuals, then their true self will be permitted to emerge, to flourish, and to grow under our appropriate, loving tutelage.

The effective parent is aware that children are "imitation machines". Children imitate whatever they see around them. So, parents, give them good examples to mimic. Be who you want your child to become. The professional parent relationship with their children is one of encouraging the child's individuation to emerge without the nagging, negative, critical inner voices.

By reading this book and doing the exercises, anyone can learn to experience more of the fun and less of the fury of family life. Read each chapter. Do the exercises. Spend time practicing the communication tools. Then you can apply what you learn to your parenting skills and begin to make some positive changes in the way your family gets along together.

Cool!

You will be able to teach these new communication skills to your children (and partner and friends), because you will be using the skills with them. You will be able to include whomever you like in this world of real, honest and clear communication. No longer will you merely be mechanical and thoughtless, repeating the same words, threats and punishments that you may have received as a child. You will be an effective communicator and peace, harmony, laughter and love will be your reward. Really. You'll see.

The Philadelphia Story
--Kaela

When I was a little girl, I grew up in Philadelphia and the winter snows were cold and blustery. One winter, when I was about six-years-old, my mother bundled me up to go outside. She dressed me in snow boots, leggings, parka, jacket, scarf, mittens and a hat. I felt and looked like the Abominable Snowman. I couldn't move. My body was baking from layers of insulation. I looked up at my mother and said, "I'm hot." She huffed, "No, you're not." I wondered whether I might be wrong. I supposed that, since she was my mother, she must be right. I still felt hot.

In order to make sure she had the information about how I felt, I said again, with the innocence of a six-year-old, "But I'm hot inside, mommy." She harrumphed more emphatically, "No, you're not. It's cold outside. You are not hot!"

That was the moment I first began to doubt my own reality.

HIGHLIGHTS

- The job of the parent is to teach children how to identify and express their needs and feelings.

- Children need an adult to take them seriously and help them behave in an age-appropriate manner.

- The job of the child is to live, laugh, love and learn.

- Parenting is a set of skills that can be learned.

- Children are imitation machines.

CHAPTER

Is The Way You Were Parented The Way You Are Parenting?

Is the Way You Were Parented the Way You Are Parenting?

~~~~~~

Our early relationships with our parents indelibly affect our lives and all the subsequent relationships we will have. In order for you to become a better parent you must first understand this because you are the child who has grown up as a product of your parenting. You will need to understand your behavior before you can help your child learn about his behavior.

Golly!

How you were parented as a child has a great deal to do with how you now communicate. If you experienced inappropriate parenting – yelling, sarcasm, name-calling or an absence of genuine attention, you may find yourself repeating the same behaviors. These behaviors were modeled for you by the adults around you during your childhood. And you have probably been imitating them. Remember, children are imitation machines. You just imitated what you saw. You thought these behaviors were acceptable. That's the way you thought the world worked.

Let's be clear. We are not bashing anyone's parents. Undoubtedly, our parents did the best they could with what they knew at the time. Today, we know a lot more about how our childhood influences affect our adulthood.

You are "you". And this "you" was formed early. About eighty percent of the concepts, notions, beliefs and ideas you call your own were in place by age eight. These came to you from your parents, authority figures, movies, TV programs, Pooh Bear, you name them.

So, in order for you to become as aware as you possibly can, we are asking you to become a student of your behavior and of your language patterns.

Inappropriate parenting sounds something like this:

Parent: *Put your coat on. It's cold outside.*

Child: *I was just outside. I didn't feel cold.*

Parent: *I said put your coat on or you can't go outside. You'll be cold.*

Reason: *Child is not cold. This is the parent's perception of cold.*

Child: *I hate my brother.*

Parent: *We don't use language like that in this house.*

Reason: *Hate is just a word. Not a behavior.*

Child: *I just tied my shoes for the first time! All by myself!*

Parent: *Well, that wasn't so hard, was it?*

Reason: *The parent is invalidating the child's effort. It was difficult to master that skill. Don't belittle the effort.*

Child: *Look at this picture I just painted.*

Parent: *You're the best artist in the world.*

Reason: *This is the parent's opinion of "best". What does the child think? Let the pride come from the kid.*

In each of these simple situations a child is having a **feeling.** Ask yourself, is the parent really listening to the child? Does the parental response validate the child's feelings?

The answer is **NO.** In each of these cases, the parent does not acknowledge or accept the feeling behind the information. In fact, the feeling is squelched. And what do you do with your own feelings when they are squelched or discounted?

Oooooooh...

You stuff your feelings down inside.

You learn to pretend the feelings aren't there. You begin to ignore them and without even knowing it, you lose trust in your own feelings. Is this what parents intend to teach their children? Of course not! But that is exactly what children learn when parents employ inappropriate language and patterns without addressing what's really happening.

This is exactly why we must learn to identify and voice our own feelings if we are really going to do this job of parenting well. That way, when we do take the step of teaching our children and partners to recognize and express their own feelings, they will honor this expression as healthy, responsible behavior because they've heard and seen you do it. Children imitate what they see.

You, like most adults, probably have feelings that have been stuffed far down inside – feelings you try to pretend are not even there. Where do those stuffed feelings go? When you're not listened to, not taken seriously, not attended to, it hurts. We don't want to feel this hurt, so we push hurt feelings as far away from our conscious mind as possible. But denying our painful feelings has consequences. We may develop insecurity, depression, uncontrollable and unidentifiable rage, eating disorders and low self-esteem.

We need to teach our children to express their needs and feelings. Whether or not we agree or are comfortable with the information, we must make *Cool!* it safe for these feelings to be expressed.

Acceptance and Agreement

There is a difference between acceptance and agreement.

Acceptance is allowing others the right to their own feelings.
Agreement means that two or more people have the same idea, position and/or feelings about the same issue.

Acceptance builds high self-esteem, communicates trust, and creates self-respect in the one who feels accepted. Children need to feel accepted. Having a different opinion or feeling about something is okay. Children need a safe atmosphere to voice their differences. We don't have to agree with each other to accept each other's feelings.

Example:

Your teenager wants his bedtime to be 11:00 pm on school

nights. You want his bedtime to be at 10:00 pm.
This is a difference of opinion.

Your 9-year-old wants to go out in fifty-degree weather with just a sweater. You want your 9-year-old to wear the hat, the scarf, the gloves and the snowsuit.
This is a difference of opinion.

Your best friend comes back from a movie date and tells you how much she loved the movie. "You've got to go see it. You'll love it!" she says. You go to see it and you hate it.
This is a difference of opinion.

People can look at a Picasso and love it or look at a Picasso and hate it.
This is a difference of opinion.

We can disagree about something without withdrawing our acceptance of the person whose opinion differs from ours. We can agree to disagree. Acceptance communicates *This rocks!* respect while acknowledging differences. Acceptance shows you how to value the other perception and allows them the right to their feelings.

Agreement means that two or more people have the same idea, position and/or feelings about the same issue. There's no doubt that agreement makes it easier to be with someone. But it is impossible for people to agree all the time. We must learn to accept differences.

Parent the Child, not the Parent

What's *Really* Going On?

This is one of the stories told to us by the mother and father of a four-year-old boy.

The father's story: When I was a toddler, I remember wanting my father's attention. I would never get it. He was an important man with business deals all over town. As I grew up, no matter how hard I tried, I just could not please him. Nothing I did ever made him happy about me. Now that I have a son of my own I am giving him attention all the time. I take him to soccer. We go riding on my motorcycle together. My wife and I have enrolled him in the best school. He's only four and he goes to school practically all day.

The mother's story: (She was sitting next to her husband and looked like she was going to cry.) We asked her "What's going on?" She responded quietly, "Our son is frightened of the motorcycle. He plays soccer, but he doesn't like it. And he complains to me every single day that school is too long."

Wow!

While the father of the young boy would have loved this kind of attention from his own father, he parents his son in a style that is not appropriate to the child in front of him. Rather he is re-parenting himself through his son.

HIGHLIGHTS

- Listen for the feelings behind the words.

- Acceptance is allowing others the right to their own feelings.

- You must accept what your child says, but you don't have to agree.

CHAPTER 2

A Clear Language

A Clear Language

In the past, when shown our child's painting, report card, video game score or whatever, we may have said, "You're great. You're brilliant! I'm so proud of you!" Believe it or not, this is a judgment about their accomplishment or behavior. A judgement can be positive or negative. "You're brilliant!" is a positive judgement. We judged them and let them know our verdict. The trouble with this is that once the verdict was passed down, our children became dependent on us for the value of themselves and their accomplishments.

Such judgments, however well-intentioned, take away the child's internal self-approval, and substitute the need for external approval. Soon the cycle is set up for the child to trust himself less and to need more and more and more approval from parents, and eventually from others. Unfortunately, it's very hard to get over that need once children feel that external approval is more important than internal approval or self-approval.

Now, if outside approval really satisfied us, that would be fine. But it doesn't. Approval must come from inside to be satisfying. If parents take it away by offering such judgments as, "You're great! You're brilliant", children lose self-trust and self-value. Children then begin to think they need to keep searching for approval outside themselves and

27

it is an endless and futile search because approval isn't outside. We have good jobs, nice cars, homes, friends, cell phone, and business titles in front of and after our names. Yet, most of us are still insecure – still looking for approval "out there." So, can you see that insecurity comes from childhood experiences of external pats on the back?

Hmmm...

> Self-worth comes from self-approval.

> Self-esteem comes from self-love.

> Self-respect comes from self-trust.

When you allow and encourage children their own feelings they say proud variations of, "I did it! I painted this picture. I achieved in this sport. I feel good about my grades." Self-esteem comes from inside.

We are going to give you the tools for this clear language. It's not tough. It just takes practice and is worth the work.

Judgments and Behaviors

Judgement is an opinion, conclusion, or decision about something. You are the judge. You have made your mind up about something, and therefore it is so. Judgement words are not helpful in describing behavior. They color the action with your own opinion about what's going on. A judgement speaks to, and often attacks, a person's character.

Notice the **judgment** words in your speech and begin to take those words out. Words like:

Rude	Irresponsible	Stupid
Clumsy	Good	Angelic
Smart	Pretty	Talented
Droopy	Helpless	Selfish
Pathetic	Ambitious	Lazy

Character is the personality, individuality, ego, nature, ethical traits, and essential quality of the self. Behavior is 'what' a person does. Character is 'who' a person is. Many of our language patterns rely on judgment words that speak to character, not behavior. More often than not, this language pattern is unspecific, ineffective and, often, quite hurtful.

These are judgment words that address character:

> *"You are a bad girl."*
>
> *"You're lazy."*
>
> *"You are irresponsible."*
>
> *"You're perfect."*
>
> *"That's stupid."*
>
> *"What a good kid."*

Whoa!

Behavior is a learned action, reaction, pattern, or habit— something you can see or hear. Behavior is the action being performed — **something you can take a picture of, videotape, or tape record.**

These are examples of **behavior:**

- A little boy running around holding a drawing he made.

- A four-year-old flailing his arms and screaming.

- Your teenager listening to loud music.

- Your partner working at a desk.

I see...

- A small child walking around with a banana peel on his head.

And, when you've removed judgment words from your communication, what should you put in their place, you ask? Instead of using a judgment word, what about simply describing what you see? Describe behavior. This will help you put on your non-judgmental hat. And there's another good reason why we want to speak in terms of behaviors rather than judgments. The reason is that behavior can be changed. Behavior is what a person does, not who a person is.

These are examples of behaviors that can be changed:

- The four-year-old flailing and screaming ... can start walking tippy-toe and singing.

- Your teenager listening to loud music ... can turn it down and do his homework.

- Your partner working at the desk ... can get up and start fixing dinner.

- The small child wearing the banana peel on his head ... can take it off his head.

Instead of making judgments, describe the behavior you see and hear. Avoid judgment words – even judgments that seem to be positive. Judgments are judgments.

What you see: New shoes on wet grass.

- Judgmental response: *"You're irresponsible."*

- Describing behavior response: *"I see new shoes on the wet grass."*

What you see: Your daughter with peanut butter on her face, crying.

- Judgmental response: *"Look what a mess you made."*

- Describing behavior response: *"I see a face with peanut butter all over it and I hear crying."*

What you see: Your child standing in front of his art project in school.

- Judgemental response: *"Wow! You are good."*

- Describing behavior response: *"I see a picture on a wall with squiggly lines and yellow circles."*

What you see: Your child sitting quietly in the back seat of the car.

- Judgmental response: *"My perfect, little angel."*

I see...

- Describing behavior response: *"I see a child sitting quietly in the back seat of the car."*

Judgments vs. Descriptions

Try this: Imagine describing the Mona Lisa. Just identify what you see.

I see an oval-faced woman with long dark hair.

I see folded hands and a dark dress.

31

I see hills in the background.

I see sky.

Now, what would judgments about the Mona Lisa sound like?

She's wearing an ugly dress.

That's a strange landscape.

There's too much brown color.

It's a good painting.

Yuck! This is art?

What are the judgment words? They are the words that indicate opinions.

ugly dress

strange landscape

too much brown color

good painting

yuck!

So, imagine your child has just brought you a painting he made. Let's say his painting is a colorful mix of lines and squiggles.

Warning! Warning! Warning! Resist all urges to say, "Oh, what a beautiful painting! I love it. You're a great artist." Those are your judgments. They may be positive, friendly judgments but let's take your opinion out and try what we did with Mona Lisa. Describe what you see.

I see a line and two blue circles.

I see a lot of orange squiggles.

I see brown lines touching each other.

Your child will respond with the delight of recognition and self-responsibility. "Yes! I made that line. I chose the light blue paint even though there was green paint. I made orange squiggles because I like orange squiggles. And that's a brown dog!" Your child will puff up with pride and importance. You are giving him the dignity of his own choices and you are validating his perception and reality. You are encouraging him to have his own self-esteem because you described what you saw and left him the integrity of his feelings and thoughts.

Since you are putting in place this new way of talking, let's remember you and your child already had a previous system. The old system has been in existence as long as you have been together. That is: if you have been saying, "Good boy" or "Good girl," your child is accustomed to this. If you have been saying, "No, do this" or "No, do that," your child is accustomed to hearing this kind of talk. When a new system is being set into motion in your home, be patient. Understand that children, like adults, don't like change, even if the change will benefit everyone. Children become accustomed to negative responses and think, "This is how it should be." Your life – the family's life – will be more fun, and more free from stress and negative consequences. But in the beginning it can be difficult to change. Remember to demonstrate patience, understanding and respect.

Think about some behaviors you've seen at your house. Practice thinking and speaking in terms of behavior, and be as detailed and specific as possible.

Yelling on the phone **behavior**

Staying out late **behavior**

Picking up clothes **behavior**

Playing with the dog **behavior**

Hugging and kissing **behavior**

Using the word "behavior" will assist your child in understanding what is going on. A child can recognize eating behavior, talking behavior, walking behavior, looking at video behavior.

When adults talk about behavior, the message that is most important for children to understand is this: behavior can change.

The child begins to understand that he is loved. This is permanent. The activities a child does are behaviors. Behaviors can change. They are impermanent.

Ah ha!

~~~~~~~~~~~~~ **EXERCISE** ~~~~~~~~~~~~~~

Take a moment and describe five behaviors that children do indoors.

_____behavior

_____behavior

_____behavior

_____behavior

_____behavior

Take another moment and describe five behaviors that children do outdoors.

_____behavior

_____behavior

_____behavior

_____behavior

_____behavior

Even a fairly young child will be able to understand you when you speak like this, because when you describe what you observe, everyone will know exactly what you are talking about – and that means you are being an effective communicator. Words like "talented", "lazy" and "rude" are vague and do not really address what is actually happening. They are ineffective attempts to communicate without really describing the behavior. Judgment words are automatic.

Automatic language is judgmental, labeling and name-calling. We want you to get away from saying anything like: "You are so lazy' or "You are so good."

Wow!

Labeling and name-calling don't describe behavior. They express your judgment. Young children don't know what you mean when you say, "You're so lazy." They do know that it's bad. They do feel wrong. And, because children's thinking is so black and white, they make themselves all bad and all wrong. When the child feels the negative judgment, it damages the self. The judgment is "judgmental language" which gets internalized and makes it very hard to change. We must teach our children that we love them all the time but we may not like their behavior. Remember, behavior can change.

Telling children what you see and hear helps them know exactly what you mean – nothing vague, nothing ambiguous. You give them information they can understand. Shoes on the floor behavior. We can all see this. No judgments, just description. Give them information that allows them to change their behavior and enjoy their own success.

Let's come up with a description of behavior that allows a child to feel smart. "I see a report card with seven categories. In every category there's an 'A'. "When you talk to a child like this he will feel good about himself. He might think or say, "I got seven 'A's. I did that. I am smart!"

If you call the child a negative name, that name is going to stick. Rude. Lazy. Ungrateful. There are feelings connected to these words. Those feelings will hang around inside your child and hurt them. Because judgment words don't give enough information, the child may not even know exactly what you mean. Great!

When you praise a child with words like "You're such a good boy", you have set up an expectation that the child must always be "good"– an expectation that cannot always be met. You have announced an expectation of the child's character, not addressed his immediate behavior.

The Case of the Flying Ashtray:
A Story with a Moral

~~~~~~

Here is a story I remember hearing in a seminar in the late 1960's. It is told from the mother's perspective.

Oh my!

The whole family was piled in the car. We had just driven four hundred miles from Pittsburgh to New York. My son John behaved like an angel in the back seat of the car. He was quiet and deep in thought. I said to myself, "He deserves some praise." As we entered the Lincoln Tunnel I turned to him and said "You are such a good boy, John. You behaved so well. I am proud of you."

A moment later the sky seemed to fall in on us as John pulled out an ashtray and spilled its contents all over us. The ashes, the cigarette butts and the smoke kept coming like atomic fallout. We were in the tunnel in heavy traffic and we were choking and coughing. I was shocked and I could have killed him. If it weren't for the witnesses in the other cars I would have murdered him on the spot. What infuriated me the most was the fact that I had just sincerely praised him. Isn't praise good for children any more?

Three weeks later John, himself, revealed the cause of his explosion. You see, all the way home he had been wondering how he could get rid of his younger brother who was happily snuggled up between his mother and father in the front seat. At last an idea occurred to him. If the car were in an accident, his brother could be thrown into the windshield while he and his parents could be safe — no more baby brother. From then on he

37

would be the one snuggling between his parents in the front seat. That was the moment that his mother congratulated him on his 'goodness'. The praise made him feel guilty. He desperately wanted to show his mom that he did not deserve the praise. He looked around, saw the ashtray, and the emotional storm followed instantly.

Begin to really focus on what you are saying to your child. Remember how we were talking about describing the behavior? Let's say the mother, instead of delivering the judgmental angel speech, had described the behavior she saw. "I see a quiet little boy, hands folded, looking out the window." That is a description that tells what she sees. It also allows for the little boy to know what she sees. In other words, the opportunity is there for him to say, "I am quietly sitting here in the back seat. But I am thinking that my brother has been in the front seat for a very long time. I would like to be sitting in the front seat between my parents instead of him."

Hmmm...

Different scenario, eh?

~~~~~~~~~~~~~~~~EXERCISE~~~~~~~~~~~~~~~~~

Practice turning the following judgement words into descriptions of behavior:

Example: Angelic– "I see a quiet little boy, hands folded, looking out the window."

Angelic: _____

Lazy: _____

Cry-baby: _____

Smarty-pants: _____

Talented: _____

~~~~~~

You have been practicing staying away from judgments and offering descriptions of what you see and hear instead — descriptions about behavior. Hopefully, you'll start to feel less upset and more objective when you offer comments like: "I see socks and shoes thrown across the carpet behavior," rather than saying, "You are so sloppy."

Awesome!

Being neutral and simply stating what we see is easier on us – and on everyone around us – no judgments, just descriptions.

With practice, this new system will make your life easier. It will also enrich your child's life because you are giving him language – no automatic response, no abbreviations, but descriptive, colorful, textured, specific, clear language. It may not be simple to remember what to do initially, but it will become second nature with practice. When we walk around unconscious – unaware of how we are speaking and what we are saying to our children, we run the risk of falling into judgmental patterns which can create confusion and negative feelings in our children. Taking control of our language makes us all much more aware of what we actually mean.

Remember, awareness is the first step to positive change. Be aware. Catch yourself when you are making judgments. Apply yourself to change your language pattern with your children. That's how you'll become a more responsible communicator who has a respectful and honest relationship with your children.

Acceptable and Unacceptable Behaviors

Acceptable behaviors are physical and verbal acts that demonstrate support, love, trust and appreciation for others.

Unacceptable behaviors are physical and verbal acts that demonstrate disrespect, distrust and a lack of appreciation for others.

It is important to become aware of other judgment words being expressed in your daily life: the use of the words "good" and "bad" to describe behavior. Instead, try using the terms "acceptable" and "unacceptable" behavior. When children hear the words "good" and "bad" they think of themselves as either *all* good or *all* bad. There are no shades of gray in a child's world. The words "acceptable" and "unacceptable" address behavior. *A child is not his behavior.*

Think of five examples of acceptable behavior you see in your home. Remember to *describe* behavior. What does "polite," "respectful," or "good manners" look like? Catch yourself when you're being automatic. We want to be clear and specific with our language. *Describe* what the acceptable behavior looks like.

Uh huh!

You will notice that each time we describe behavior (shoes on the bed behavior, dishes in the sink behavior, talking on the phone behavior, etc.) we keep stating the word "behavior". Granted, it's not the King's English, but in order for us to begin thinking in terms of identifying behavior instead of attacking character, it helps to say that word over and over to ourselves and our children.

Examples:
Bouncing balls together outside behavior
Working on your homework with extra time to spare behavior
Riding skateboards in the driveway behavior
CD-listening behavior
Lunch-making the night before school behavior

Describe your examples of acceptable behavior:

_____behavior

_____behavior

_____behavior

_____behavior

_____behavior

Think of five examples of unacceptable behavior in your home. Remember, "mean," "nasty," and "uncooperative" are not descriptive behaviors – it is using judgmental language. How about ... ?
Hitting behavior
Screaming behavior
Leaving food out after lunch behavior
Smacking your brother in the head with a hard toy behavior

Describe your examples of unacceptable behavior:

_____behavior

_____behavior

_____behavior

_____behavior

_____behavior

~~~~~~

Can you hear how "Don't be stupid!" differs from "I see unacceptable hitting of your brother on the head with a hard toy behavior." Say this while you are stopping the behavior and protecting the brother. The sentence that talks about what is actually happening delivers so much more information. Here's the information the child receives: Hitting is unacceptable behavior.

Determining Acceptable or Unacceptable Behavior When "The Self" Changes

~~~~~~

You're in a great mood, just got a raise, bought a new outfit and are on your way to the movies tonight. You get home and your teenager is blasting rock music. It's coursing through the house. But you're in a great mood so it's no problem.

On a another day, you get laid off, have an accident with an uninsured car, and when you get home your teenager is blasting rock music — the same song — throughout the house. The same behavior is now unacceptable behavior.

Acceptable/Unacceptable Behavior
When the "Other Person" Changes.

~~~~~~

Your five-year-old wants to ride his bike to school alone and school is a quarter of a mile away. That is unacceptable behavior.

Your thirteen-year-old wants to ride his bike to school alone and he is bike-safe, will wear a helmet and is traveling to a school a quarter of a mile away. That sounds like acceptable behavior.

Hmmm...

Acceptable/Unacceptable Behavior
When the "Setting" Changes

~~~~~~

Your five-year-old is *outside* engaged in bouncing the ball behavior. **Acceptable.**

Your five-year-old is *inside* standing on the new floor engaged in bouncing the ball behavior. **Unacceptable.**

We see that the line between acceptable and unacceptable behavior can change.

I 'm Not Cold. Oh, Yes You Are!

~~~~~~

When I was a young therapist I had a nine-year old girl as a client. She came into my practice with her mother. The nine-year old always arrived at my office dressed in shorts in the summer and winter. One day we talked about trusting our own feelings and acknowledging and expressing them.

At the end of the session the young girl began walking toward the door. Her mother admonished her, "Put on your sweater, it's cold outside." The youngster opened the door, felt the air for herself, and turned to her mom and said, "I'm not cold." The mother repeated, "It's cold outside. Put on your sweater." Her daughter responded, "But Mom, I'm not cold." Angry now, her mother responded through gritted teeth, "If you don't put your sweater on right now I'm taking your television privileges away for a whole week. And you can't play with the cat. No telephone either."

This mother was so overwhelmed by her need to be right that she used her parental authority to intimidate her daughter.

I pointed out to both of them that the child's temperature gauge was vastly different from her mother's. And perhaps it would be a good idea for the mother to validate that difference to her child.

Here's how the scenario might have played out:

> Mother standing at the door, "Put on your sweater because it's cold outside."
>
> Daughter, opening the door feeling the temperature for herself, "It doesn't feel cold to me." The mother

responds, "Oh, it doesn't feel cold to you? I have your sweater here so I'll carry it. If it feels cold to you later you can put it on."

The daughter feels validated, included, and respected. Her self-esteem and self-reliance have been encouraged. The mother feels as if she has done her best job at listening and validating her child. Because her daughter was heard and validated she was able to experience her own need to carry a sweater in case of a change of temperature.

HIGHLIGHTS

- Self-worth comes from self-approval. Self-esteem comes from self-love. Self-respect comes from self-trust.

- Automatic language is judgmental language.

- Positive-sounding judgment words are still judgment words.

- Describe what you see and hear, without judgment.

- Behavior is something you can videotape or take a picture of.

- Behavior can change.

- Recognize the difference between acceptable and unacceptable behaviors, and the factors that affect them.

CHAPTER 3

The Importance Of Feelings

The Importance of Feelings

A **feeling** is a physical response to a particular situation or a particular sensation. The brain interprets a feeling through thought and language. Feelings remind us that we are alive.

This Rocks!

The more we can recognize and state our feelings clearly, the more we can know what is going on within ourselves. The ability to identify and communicate our feelings responsibly helps us to be conscious of the truth.

Conversely, when we deny, avoid, stuff down, manipulate, and/or hide from our feelings, we are hiding from the truth. When we hide from the truth, we cannot respond responsibly to the world around us. Suppressed feelings, stuffed down, eventually begin to escape and can cause us to behave irrationally and irresponsibly.

For example: Anger is a secondary emotion. The primary emotions that cause anger are hurt and fear. When these original emotions are denied we respond with the emotion of anger. Then, when anger is not expressed responsibly, these feelings turn to rage. If children were permitted to express their anger there would be no more rage in the world. Feelings have a life cycle, and need to be expressed.

Differences Between
Feelings and Thoughts

~~~~~~

A **thought** is a concept, an idea, a notion or a whim. It is cogitation, cerebration, speculation and consideration. It is *brainwork*.

A **feeling** is a tactile sense. A feeling is *body work*. It is a touch, a sensation, an emotion, a passion, a gut response. A feeling is not a concept. It happens inside your body, not inside your brain. A feeling is not up for discussion. It cannot be judged. It is neither good nor bad. You are not a victim of your feelings.

Ah ha!

If you feel you want to punch someone in the face, throw them on the ground and rip out their hair, you do not have to act out that feeling. What you have to do is acknowledge that you are having a feeling. What you have to do is address the sensation, the gut response that you're feeling in language that is responsible, clear and passionate. Also, if you feel like jumping up on a stage and kissing a performer or a president, you are still not at the mercy of that feeling. You can acknowledge it. You can feel it. You can hold it. You can enjoy it. And, again, you are not at the mercy of your feelings. Your feelings belong to you.

Many times people communicate a feeling as a thought. It sounds like this:

I feel like hitting you.

I feel like not talking any more.

I feel like pulling my hair out.

I feel like you don't understand me.

Here may be the real feelings:

I feel angry. (I feel like hitting you.)

I feel frustrated. (I feel like not talking anymore.)

I feel panic-stricken. (I feel like pulling my hair out.)

I feel upset. (I feel as if you don't understand me.)

EXAMPLE

Your wife is always late. You say, "I feel as if you shouldn't be late all the time." What the husband has described is what he thinks about his wife being late. He says, "I feel," but he never talks about his feelings. He only talks about his thoughts as if they are his feelings.

How the husband feels could be hurt, unimportant and discounted. The communication would be much clearer if the husband could say, "When you are late for a date with me I feel hurt, unimportant and discounted." Now he is talking about his feelings.

Feelings are just feelings. It is not necessary to act on them. Address them, identify them, and if appropriate, discharge them responsibly by talking about them without pointing a finger or blaming the other person. The irresponsible expression of feelings sounds like blaming, yelling, insulting and name calling.

Watch out when people say, "You shouldn't feel that way" or "You should feel this way." No one can tell you if your feeling is good, bad, right or wrong. It is your feeling. No opinion about it can matter.

The Language of Feelings

Some parents may worry that by encouraging children to talk about their feelings they are encouraging them to wallow in sad feelings or teaching them to be overly emotional.

In our experience, even a child's strongest feelings do not last long after they are released and talked about. On the other hand, when a child's feelings are not given space, when they are "stuffed," this can cause those feelings to last a long time. And children's feelings are just as real and valid as adults' feelings. Stuffing feelings is not healthy for anyone of any age. In fact, stuffing feelings can mean the difference between anger and rage. When anger is ignored, it becomes powerful, loud, and scary — it becomes rage. Rage is much harder to deal with than anger because it's bigger and deeper. It breathes fire, *Wow!* has big hairy horns, and its eyes are red. Rage is dangerous!

Ideally, we want to encourage children to voice their feelings. What's the most effective way to do that? By giving them the language of feelings. Asked to identify feelings people usually only come up with a few: sad, glad, mad, angry, happy and frustrated. Are those the only feelings that we have? We don't think so. Take a look at the following list:

Feelings aren't good or bad, they're just feelings.

Abandoned	Bitter	Contrite
Able	Blissful	Coolness
Abominable	Bold	Cowardly
Adamant	Bored	Crippled
Adequate	Brave	Cruel
Affectionate	Broken	Crushed
Agony	Burdened	Culpable
Alarm	Calm	Deceitful
Almighty	Capable	Defeated
Altruistic	Captivated	Deficient
Ambivalent	Challenged	Dejected
Amorous	Charmed	Delighted
Angry	Charming	Deluded
Anguish	Cheated	Demoralized
Annoyed	Cheerful	Desirous
Anxious	Childish	Despair
Apathetic	Clever	Despise
Astounded	Combative	Destructive
Aversion	Competent	Determined
Awed	Competitive	Detest
Bad	Concern	Devotion
Baffled	Confident	Different
Balk	Confounded	Diffident
Beautiful	Confused	Diminished
Betrayed	Conspicuous	Disabled
Bewildered	Contented	Disappointment

Discontent	Fascinated	Hateful
Dislike	Fawning	Healthy
Displeased	Fearful	Heavenly
Distaste	Fearless	Helpful
Distracted	Feeble	Helpless
Distraught	Flustered	High
Disturbed	Fondness	Homesick
Divided	Foolish	Honored
Dominated	Fortunate	Horrible
Doubtful	Frantic	Horrified
Dread	Free	Hostile
Dubious	Fright	Hurt
Eager	Frightened	Hysterical
Ecstatic	Frustrated	Ignored
Effective	Full	Immortal
Electrified	Furious	Important
Empty	Gay	Imposed
Enchanted	Genuine	Impotent
Energetic	Glad	Impressed
Enervated	Gloomy	Incompetent
Enjoy	Gratified	Ineffective
Envious	Greedy	Infatuated
Evil	Grief	Inferior
Exasperated	Groovy	Infuriated
Excited	Guilty	Injured
Exhausted	Gullible	Inspired
Exposed	Happy	Intimidated
Failure	Harassed	Irritated

Isolated	Misgivings	Pleasant
Jealous	Mixed-up	Pleased
Joyful	Mournful	Powerful
Joyous	Mystical	Powerless
Jumpy	Naughty	Precarious
Keen	Nervous	Pressured
Kicky	Nervy	Pretty
Kind	Nice	Prim
Laconic	Obnoxious	Prissy
Lazy	Obsessed	Proud
Lecherous	Odd	Puzzled
Left Out	Odious	Quarrelsome
Licentious	Odium	Queer
Likable	Offended	Quiet
Loathe	Opposed	Rage
Lonely	Outraged	Rapture
Longing	Overwhelmed	Refreshed
Loving	Pain	Rejected
Low	Panicked	Rejection
Lucky	Paralyzed	Relaxed
Lustful	Parsimonious	Relieved
Mad	Passion	Remorse
Maudlin	Peaceful	Repel
Mean	Peerless	Repugnant
Meek	Perplexed	Resentful
Melancholy	Persecuted	Restless
Merry	Petrified	Reverent
Miserable	Pity	Rewarded

Righteous	Strong	Uncertain
Robust	Stuffed	Uneasy
Sad	Stunned	Unhappy
Sated	Stupefied	Unimportant
Satisfied	Stupid	Unsatisfied
Scared	Suffering	Unsure
Screwed-up	Sure	Useless
Secure	Sympathetic	Vehement
Self-absorbed	Talkative	Vexed
Self-assured	Tearful	Violent
Sensitive	Tempted	Vital
Servile	Tenacious	Vitality
Settled	Tenderness	Vivacious
Sexy	Tense	Vulnerable
Shocked	Tentative	Weak
Silly	Tenuous	Weepy
Skeptical	Terrible	Wicked
Small	Terrified	Wonderful
Sneaky	Terror	Worried
Solemn	Threatened	Wrathful
Sore	Thwarted	Zany
Sorrowful	Tired	
Spiteful	Torment	
Stable	Tormented	
Startled	Trapped	
Stingy	Troubled	
Strange	Ugly	

And that's just *some* of the "feeling" vocabulary. Isn't this a marvelous list? Bold, energetic, communicative! We all experience all of these feelings. Don't just say "happy" — elaborate! Enough with the "sad". Be expressive! Make a genuine effort to use these specific empowering words. Your children will catch on quicker than you can spell "exuberant".

EXAMPLE

Your ten-year-old is going to sleep-away camp for the first time and says, "Will anyone I know be there?"

What might your child be feeling? Think about the situation. Imagine what your child might be feeling...Scared? Worried? Uneasy? Yes, these are a few of the feelings the child probably is experiencing.

Now look at these following comments and questions. Let's see what feelings the following speakers might have. Again, using the feeling list, what might the speaker be experiencing?

"Do you think we're going to have any more big earthquakes?" How might the speaker be feeling? Anxious, vulnerable, concerned, powerless?

"Dad never plays with us any more. He's too busy." How might the speaker be feeling here? Annoyed, alone, disappointed, ignored, abandoned?

"This is the second time I'm taking my driving test." How might the speaker be feeling? Nervous, confused, unsure?

Look at the number of feeling words we've just introduced: abandoned, alone, annoyed, anxious, concerned, confused, disappointed, excited, ignored, nervous, powerless, unsure, vulnerable.

We can now give all these wonderful words to our own children. It's like giving them all the different colored crayons in the box. By giving them the vocabulary of feelings they will be able to identify and responsibly deal with all of the emotions that they have. There really are oodles of specific, textured feeling words that we need to recognize and identify to help both ourselves and our children.

Sure!

Decoding Messages

Understand that children speak in coded messages. Children need help in decoding their communication. Often, without help, they can't get to the bottom of what they mean to say. We need to give them the way to uncover their true feelings and speak about them.

So, let's say your child comes to you with strong feelings. It may sound as simple as:

I don't want to go to school today.

Daddy, don't go to work.

I don't like recess.

I hate my brother.

Decode the message and identify the REAL feeling:

Message   *Feeling*

I don't want to go to school today. *anxious* _____

Daddy, don't go to work.   _____

I don't like recess.   _____

I hate my brother.   _____

"I'm not shy, Mommy."

One day, when Cydney was four or five, we went shopping in the supermarket. We were picking out the vegetables. We were picking out the cereal. We were having a good time being together in the supermarket. And then, **IT** happened again.

Because Cydney was a pretty little girl, most of her life people would come over and say, "My, what a pretty girl you are." This day was no different. Three or four people wanted to admire and touch her as we cruised down the aisles. My daughter would turn away and look in the other direction to avoid the person's eyes or touch.

I politely explained to the people that she was shy. Some smiled and reached out to pat her head. Each time, I explained, "She's shy". In the checkout line another person came over, reached for my daughter and said, "Oh, what a lovely face you have. You're so beautiful." My daughter turned her shoulder and moved away. I addressed the woman and said, "She's shy".

When the lady wandered off Cydney looked up at me and said, "Mommy, I'm not shy."

Puzzled, I asked, "Oh, you're not shy?"

"No," she said, "I'm not shy. I just don't like being touched by strangers."

Wow. That was a big lesson for me. I interpreted her behavior the way *I* perceived it.

I learned my lesson, so when the next person came close and commented on her beauty and my daughter pulled away, I said, "She doesn't like being touched by strangers." The stranger took his hands away and smiled at her. She smiled back. At last, she felt validated and heard.

HIGHLIGHTS

• There are differences between feelings and thoughts.

• Help your child use the language of feelings.

• Look for the feelings behind the words.

• Look for the real meaning in children's coded messages.

CHAPTER 4

All About Pickles

Replace Problems with Pickles

The word "problem" has a lot of baggage attached to it. It's a heavy, negative word. When you hear it you automatically think: "solve it" or "fix it." Often this is not the best thing to do. That's why, from now on in this workbook, we'll be using the word *pickle* to mean a situation about which you or your child, has strong feelings. We have decided to lighten up the word *problem* and have chosen to replace it with the word *pickle*. We illustrate this concept with "The Pig Family Pickles", cause, who's afraid of the big bad pickle???!!

When you change the way you talk about a situation, you upgrade the opportunity to change your mindset. If I say, "That's your *pickle*", I'd like you to think you have a predicament, a muddle, a concern, something that isn't the way you want it to be — but without the heavy burden of "having a problem." When you use the word *pickle* to refer to many of the issues that confront parents and children every day, the lightness of the word helps you keep the ups and downs of family life in perspective. Humor and a playful approach are often a positive way to begin addressing a *pickle*. Even the most serious *pickles* can be dealt with effectively when you use the techniques in this workbook.

In this chapter, you will learn how to determine whether a particular situation is a real *pickle,* and whether it's your *pickle* or your child's *pickle.*

This Rocks!

You need to know whose *pickle* it is before you can decide which communication technique will be the most effective to use in addressing the *pickle.*

Children need to be taught by their parents how to look inside themselves and how to deal with their own feelings so that they can come up with solutions to their own *pickles.* Children who are not dependent on someone else to solve *pickles* for them are armed against peer pressure and are better able to cope with the complicated demands of modern society.

What we're trying to do is teach children how to become self-reliant, have self-esteem, and self-awareness so that when something difficult comes up and a parent is not around, they will have the tools to cope appropriately.

Wow! Golly! Gee!

It may be that in your family your parents either took over your *pickles* for you ("Here's what you should do"), or tried to make you feel you didn't have a *pickle* after all ("Don't worry about that"). We want to learn to deal with our own *pickles* ourselves so we can teach our children how to identify and deal with their own *pickles.* Here's how we do that...

You can place all behavior that occurs in your environment somewhere within the Action Circle (see illustration). We've chosen this particular design because it demonstrates the idea that your *pickle* and their *pickle* are often part of each other. When you care about someone, their pickles concern you, and your pickles concern them. However, if you cannot learn to identify whose *pickle* it is, you may actually hinder the other's chance for resolution.

Each specific behavior that occurs in your family is either acceptable or unacceptable. If someone else's actions are unacceptable to you, you have the *pickle*. "I hate it when I'm interrupted on the phone!" Your *pickle*. Your child comes in and his lower lip is quivering and a tear falls from his eye. He has the *pickle*. Let's look at each of these examples in turn.

When the particular behavior that's taking place is acceptable to you and your child, that behavior belongs in the **No *Pickle* Zone of the Action Circle.**

Our intention for this workbook is to help you and your family to increase the size of the No *Pickle* Zone. Examples of behaviors that are *acceptable* to you:

Your child is watching television after finishing his homework.

Your teenager is talking on the phone with her schoolmate.

Your kindergartner is racing to get ready for carpool.

Your child chooses a third book to be read at bedtime.

It's easy to see why these behaviors might belong in the No *Pickle* Zone. Everything is running smoothly, no one is unhappy, no one's behavior is impeding anyone else's and no one's needs are going unmet.

Describe in a few words some of the behaviors that occur in your household that fit in the No Pickle Zone.

1. _____

2. _____

3. _____

4. _____

Action Circle

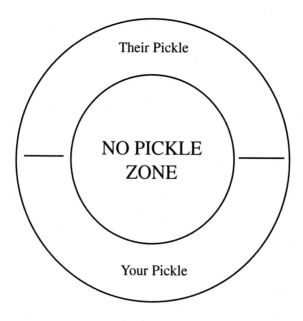

Whose Pickle Is It?

How do you know whose *pickle* it is? One way is to look at who is experiencing the strongest feeling about this *pickle*—is it your child or is it you? The person who comes in with the most energy and the loudest noise level is usually the person whose *pickle* it is.

Remember, children talk in coded messages. They often have feelings without knowing what they are. This causes them to act out. Your child comes in and tosses his lunchbox on the ground, saying, "I'm not going to school tomorrow!" That's a coded message.

Our job as parents is to figure out the coded message, understand what the *pickle* is, and determine whose *pickle* it is.

If it's the child's *pickle,* that means that you identify it, and use the tool that will *Awesome!* facilitate communication. And once you and your child begin talking about the behavior it will give him a chance to describe what is going on.

Let me clearly state that if your child is bleeding from any part of his body, now is NOT the time to discuss the *pickle,* it may be time to call 911! If a behavior is hurtful to someone else the harmful action must be halted. If this is not the appropriate time to address the feeling behind the child's *pickle,* you must inform him that you both will need to talk about this later. However, you must remember to keep your word and have the *pickle* discussion as soon as time is available.

Wow!

What about when your child is hurting emotionally? You hurt too, right? Does that make it your *pickle?* No. Observe that you're taking on his *pickle,* but it's still his. In order to help our children grow up to be whole and emotionally healthy, we must permit them their feelings, listen to them, and create a safe space for their feelings to be expressed. Simply be there. Listening to your child will encourage communication to flow.

It's Your Child's Pickle When...

EXAMPLES:

Your preschooler bursts into tears while watching a scary video.

Your daughter finds herself the object of teasing at school because she isn't very athletic. She tells you, "I'm just a total loser at everything that counts!"

Your child has just begun kindergarten and will no longer go to sleep alone in his bed without a lot of delaying tactics.

Your thirteen-year-old daughter has two pimples on her face, one of them right on her nose. On the evening of a school dance she keeps looking in the mirror and wailing, "I'm hideous!"

Your 7-year-old child has been invited to a slumber party, but he can't decide what to wear, what to pack, or even if he should go. He keeps putting things in his backpack and taking them out again, all the while asking you questions like, "What if I have to go to the bathroom in the middle of the night?

Every situation is new when you're a child. Your children are encountering so many events they've never had to deal with before. They're going to school. They're interacting with teachers and other authority figures. They're trying to make friends. They're taking tests. They're playing video games and watching TV and finding out what's going on in the world. They're feeling embarrassed and awkward if they don't know the right answers and appropriate behaviors.

From birth to age four your children learn how to sleep, eat, sit, walk, play and talk. From the ages of four to nine *It's not easy!* your children learn how to interact with other children and adults, how to have a sense of humor, how to compete and how to deal with both winning and losing. It's not easy. They're having new feelings all day long, feelings which they can't always identify.

That's why they need a safe arena at home where they can talk and learn to express these feelings.

Often, when children are upset or sad, they become less communicative. In cases like this, you must look for non-verbal cues, such as crying, pouting or withdrawing. A teenager, for example, may stop taking phone calls from friends. A younger child may not be able to fall asleep, sleep a lot, have bad dreams, or act out his distress by picking on his little brother more than usual. Some youngsters may not be dressing with the same care they usually take.

Sometimes your child may hint at his *pickle* verbally, but in an indirect way, such as saying, "I hate my sister!" Some children take their distress out on their parents by complaining about everything else but the real issue, or by criticizing everything their parents do.

Observe your child. Watch what's happening. You'll learn to recognize your own child's unique cues if you look.

When It's <u>Your</u> Pickle

~~~~~~

Sometimes it's <u>your</u> *pickle.* That's the situation when <u>you</u> are the one with the strong emotions that are running rampant, when you're not getting your needs met, or when you aren't feeling as though you're being heard. When a certain behavior on the part of your child is unacceptable to you, it's <u>your</u> *pickle.*

The way you deal with a *pickle* that's yours is, first of all, to stop, look inside yourself and say, "What's going on here?" Because you, just like a child, will find yourself acting out unless you stop and identify what's happening. By identifying your own *pickle*, you will demonstrate to your children how to identify their own pickles. It's called *modeling.*

We may have been taught by our own parents that it's not right to take the time to figure out our feelings. Perhaps they didn't have the time to teach us. More likely, they didn't know about the importance of self-esteem. They didn't know how to identify and express their own feelings. They didn't know it was okay to talk about feelings because their parents didn't know, and *their* parents didn't know, and so on back through the generations.

When a child expressed an opinion that was different from the parent's opinion, it used to be called *back-talk.* We're here to learn how to give our children the tools to identify their own feelings and *pickles* so, ultimately, they can solve their own *pickles* by themselves. Otherwise, every *pickle* in the family becomes the parents' *pickle* to solve. We want to teach our children to listen and respect themselves and other people.

Here are some clear examples of when the *pickle* belongs to the parent:

- *Your teen is playing the stereo so loud that you can't take your usual Saturday afternoon nap.*

- *Your 4-year-old is pouring water all over the bathroom floor in the process of "feeding" his plastic tub animals.*

- *Your teen promised she'd be home from her friend's house at 11:00 pm and it's now midnight.*

- *Your toddler refuses to use the potty, and the nursery school you want to enroll him in requires children to be potty-trained.*

- *Your 8-year-old will not let you talk uninterrupted on the telephone.*

Through years of conditioning many of us have learned to solve our problems/*pickles* by blaming others. This book is about learning to take responsibility, which is the opposite of blaming.

We begin to take responsibility by identifying the *pickle*. If it's your *pickle* it doesn't mean the other person is not involved. We're loving, concerned people who have to participate in one another's *pickles*. However, right now we're teaching you only how to identify whose *pickle* it is so that later on you can apply the appropriate communication techniques.

List a few of your child's behaviors that you want to change, which means they fit in the YOUR PICKLE area of the diagram.

Your child doesn't turn off the computer at the agreed upon time.

_____

_____

_____

_____

While reading the following situations, ask yourself: Who has unmet needs? If you think the behavior means the other person has the pickle write a "T" in the box for "Their" pickle. If you think the behavior is causing you to have the pickle, then write an "M" in the box for "My" pickle. If you think the behavior is not an issue at all, write and "N" in the box for "No" pickle.

After you have completed the exercise, check your responses against the answers that follow.

1. You're in a hurry to get out the door, so you start to put your preschooler's sweater on him. He says angrily: "I want to do it myself!"
2. Your youngster is walking around the house with a banana peel on his head.
3. Your 4-year-old son forgot your birthday.
4. Your teenage daughter forgot your birthday.
5. Your 8-year-old won't tell you what he did in school when you ask him.
6. Your child is sad because you can't take him to school today.
7. Your child's friend destroys the train tracks your child has been building.
8. Your child cries when you wash his hair.
9. Your child often "forgets" to put all his toys away.

ANSWERS TO EXERCISE

1. T. Your child is angry. He's having the feeling first.
2. N. This is not a *pickle* at all. Your child is simply playing.
3. M. Your feelings are hurt. It's your *pickle*.
4. M. It's still your *pickle*, since you're the one who feels unloved. You may even feel worse with an older child, since you've come to expect thoughtfulness by this age.
5. N. If you're curious about what your child did at school and he won't respond to your curiosity, there isn't a *pickle*.
6. T. Your child has the *pickle*. He needs help dealing with his feelings.
7. T   Your child is upset because his tracks have been messed up. It's his *pickle*.
8. T. Your child is unhappy. It's his *pickle*.
9. M. You're frustrated. It's your *pickle*.

We spend a lot of time discussing how to determine who has a particular *pickle* because you need that information in order to choose the most effective tool to deal with the *pickle*. The goal is to move more and more of your child's behavior into the **No *Pickle* Zone**. That's the place in which all members of the family can live, laugh, love and grow most peacefully.

You achieve the **No *Pickle* Zone** through effective, responsible and on-going communication.

Am I Invisible?

~~~~~~

Every Friday night for 5 1/2 years at 7:30 in the evening a married couple, Kaela (yes,me) and Arnold (my late husband), received a telephone call from Arnold's father. It went something like this:

Kaela:	*(Picks up the phone)* Hello.
Dad:	Hello, Kaela.
Kaela:	Hello, Dad!
Dad:	How are you?
Kaela:	Fine!
Dad:	That's nice. Is Arnold there?

Kaela feels invisible, unheard, and uncared about. Wanting to express herself to Arnold, she says:

Kaela *(to Arnold)*:	It doesn't feel like your father really cares about me.
Arnold *(to Kaela):*	What do you mean? He calls every Friday night.
Kaela:	But I don't think he hears me or listens to me. He's just waiting to get you on the telephone.
Arnold:	I don't know what you mean?

It was 7:30 on Friday night. The phone rang. Arnold and Kaela looked at each other. She gestured for him to listen. She picked up the phone, knowing it was her father-in-law and said:

Kaela:	Hello
Dad:	Hello, Kaela
Kaela:	Hello, Dad.
Dad:	How are you?
Kaela:	I have cancer.
Dad:	That's nice. Is Arnold there?

HIGHLIGHTS

- Problems are less scary when they're called pickles.

- Determine who's got the pickle.

- Non-verbal cues can point to pickles.

- Effective communication leads to life in the No Pickle Zone.

- Stop blaming and take responsibility.

CHAPTER

5

How To Listen So Children Will Feel Heard

How to Listen so Children
Will Feel Heard

If children do not feel heard they feel passed over, ignored, unimportant and rejected. Unfortunately, it often seems like listening has become a dying art. You and your children are in a positive and nurturing relationship, one which you value and want to keep. In order to do this you must listen to one another. People who were listened to in childhood, and treated with respect, honesty and empathy, grow up to have self-esteem. They treat themselves respectfully and feel self-reliant. They are capable of using their personal power to listen, support and value others in the same way they have learned to value themselves.

Wow!

In the early 1960's psychologists such as Haim Ginott, Alice Miller and Thomas Gordon conducted studies on communication. Their findings showed that certain techniques, used properly, created better, stronger and smoother relationships. One of these techniques is called **Active Listening**. Active Listening is the process that goes on instinctively between a parent and an infant. You have used it many times. But you didn't know that this valuable tool can also be used in all social relationships throughout your life.

Remember those wonderful sweet days when your children were just babies? When they cried you held them, patted their backs, and asked if they were hungry, wet, etc. You were actively listening, really tuning in to their needs. But a funny thing happened. As soon as they began to form words your listening stopped. Many parents used irresponsible ways to communicate with their children and began to yell, hit or ignore them. Since children mirror the behavior that they see, they will also grow up yelling, hitting and ignoring. But it's not too late to change. You can relearn communication techniques even if your baby is six-foot-three.

Hip Hip Hooray!

Listen for Understanding

Listening to your children is the most important skill you can learn. In fact, it can be a matter of life and death. Children who are not heard and not encouraged to express their feelings may end up suppressing those feelings down inside themselves and pretending they're not there — sometimes, with tragic consequences.

Children need parents who take them seriously and act appropriately. We have to help our children feel respected and validated. Feeling heard is one of the most important gifts people can share with one another. Look into your own life. Do you feel heard? Do you feel that the person listening on the other side of the table is really hearing what you are saying or, are they just waiting for you to finish so they can voice their own ideas? How was it for you in your childhood? Did the grown-ups in your life listen to you?

There are tools that will enable you to listen effectively to your children. Anyone can learn these skills. You don't have to be a mother, a father, or a grandparent. You just have to be concerned about communication. And you have to be concerned about yourself as well. Because if you learn how to listen you can teach others. You can set the standard for communication in your family. They will learn from you. Then you will feel heard.

Hmmmm!

Set Up For Active Listening

There are several steps to Active Listening. that indicate to the speaker (be they child or adult) that you are prepared to have a real conversation.

The first component is **paying attention.** This means putting down what you are doing and engaging with the speaker. If the speaker is a child, get down on his eye level so he is comfortable talking with you. Don't make him talk up to you. Check your body language – no crossed arm behavior, please. No scowling. You are about to listen with care, let your body reflect this.

Active Listening requires three things: *understanding, receptivity* and *sincerity.*

Understanding gives you the ability to put yourself in the other person's shoes. You comprehend what is being expressed. You grasp the importance of the idea being communicated. You can empathize with the speaker's situation.

Receptivity means that you receive the other person's information about their own experience even if you do not agree with it. Receptivity means you believe, trust and have confidence in the other. It creates an atmosphere for the development of responsibility. It communicates respect and builds self-esteem. Receptivity doesn't question another's judgment, opinion or worth.

Sincerity means that you truly care to listen to this person. You are there for them at this time. Sincerity demands pure attention, eye contact and time. If, for some good reason, you cannot listen when someone asks to be heard, you may communicate that you are not available at this time.

It is receptive and sincere behavior to say: "Right now is not a good time. I cannot give you my full attention. I can talk about this in ten minutes." If you are speaking to a child and this is the case, use your descriptive words: "I will be able to talk to you as soon as this phone call is over, and that will be when the big hand on the clock gets to the six at the bottom of the circle of numbers."

Here's another example of being sincere: If you are having strong feelings at the same time someone else is, it may not be a good time for you to try to Active Listen to them. They are having a *Pickle,* but so are you. You will probably not be able to put your feelings aside and be an effective listener. It is responsible to explain this and to wait *This Rocks!* until you can concentrate before you Actively Listen to them.

When you are sincere with your children and genuinely there for them, they will grow to trust you. *Treat your children like the people you want them to become, and they will.* If you say you'll be free to talk in ten minutes, be free to talk in ten minutes... or nine. If you say you will be back in five minutes, then do it. Keep your word. Don't we all want to keep our word in relationships? Yes! So, do it.

Initiating Active Listening

Active Listening is a tool to facilitate communication. You are engaged in Active Listening when the other person presents you with a pickle and you know it's their *pickle* not yours. You pay close attention. Again, Active Listening creates an environment of trust. When you Actively Listen, you are involved in the conversation and you demonstrate it to the speaker. You show that you hear what the person says and acknowledge that they have the *pickle*. You interact at eye level. Active Listening demonstrates that you care.

As you begin to Active Listen, and as you begin to integrate this clear language into your daily life, your relationships will grow and deepen. People will want to talk to you. That's because when you Active Listen, people feel that you are a trusted friend. Trust is a big, wonderful responsibility. Count yourself lucky. Isn't knowing what your child is thinking and feeling so much better than not knowing?

The purpose of Active Listening is to allow the speaker to discharge strong feelings.

Active Listening Tools

Step 1:   You say: "Did I hear you say"…

Step 2:   You mirror facts and feelings. Tell them what you <u>think</u> you hear.

EXAMPLES:

Child: *Mommy, I don't want to go to school today. It's raining.*

Mother: *Did I hear you say you don't want to go to school today because it's raining?*

Child: *Yes, I don't want to go to school today. It's raining so we won't be able to go to the zoo.*

Mother: *Might you be feeling disappointed?*

Child: *Yes. I'm disappointed. I really wanted to see the elephants.*

The reason you ask, "Did I hear you say ... ?" is to allow for misunderstanding. Sometimes, we only *think* we hear what the child is saying. Sometimes, the child says one thing and really means another. Repeating what you thought you heard allows the child to hear himself again. If it's not what he meant, he can correct it.

The reason you ask, "Might you be feeling ... ?" is because no one likes to be told what they are feeling. What you are doing is suggesting a possible feeling. If it is correct, the child can learn how to articulate it. If it is incorrect, both the child and you will be able to clarify and correct. This is called a communication. Communication is talking about *the* topic. Conversation is talking about many topics.

EXAMPLES:

Child: *Mommy, I don't want to go to school today. It's raining.*

Mother:	*Did I hear you say you don't want to go to school today because it's raining?*
Child:	*Yes. I don't want to go to school today. It's raining so we won't be able to go to the zoo.*
Mother:	*Might you be feeling disappointed?*
Child:	*No, I'm sad. I really wanted to see the elephants.*

Notice that the mother reflected what she thought she heard, suggested a possible feeling the child might be experiencing and, in doing so, allowed the child to experience the feeling. Notice also that the feeling the mother offered was not quite right. The child corrected it. As you mirror the facts and suggest a possible feeling, you help the child do it for himself. Now the proper parental response continues:

Door Openers

The above example illustrates an open-ended invitation to share more about the experience the child is feeling. It says to the child: I would like to engage in conversation. I'm interested in you. What you are saying is important to me.

Door Openers invite the speaker to expand on what is being said:

- *I would like to hear more about it.*
- *Say more about that.*
- *Tell me more.*
- *Aha.*

91

EXAMPLES:

Mother: *Oh, you're feeling sad? You really wanted to see the elephants. I would like to hear more about that.*

Child: *Well, the elephants are so big. We were drawing pictures of them in school, and I wanted to draw the elephant.*

Mother: *Uh huh....*

Child: *I wanted to see the elephant eating peanuts. I wanted to see what color the elephant is so I can draw him.*

Mother: *Aha...So you wanted to see the elephant eating peanuts and see him so you could draw him? I'd like to hear more about it.*

Child: *I'm going to draw an elephant at school today. And I'm going to color it blue.*

Acknowledgements

Acknowledgements let the speaker know that the listener is hearing.

They might sound like this:
- *Hmm*
- *Mmm ...*
- *I see ...*
- *Yes ...*

Lead-ins

A variety of expressions are useful to employ when you begin to use your Active Listening techniques. Here are some phrases that are helpful when you trust that your perceptions are accurate and that the child is receptive to your Active Listening.

- *From your point of view...*
- *As you see it....*
- *Do you believe...?*
- *It seems to you...*
- *Do you think ... ?*

EXAMPLE:

Child: *I did turn off the computer at 9:30.*
Mother: *It seems to you the computer was turned off at 9:30.*

Other Useful Phrases

These phrases can be used when you are unsure about what the child is saying, or if it seems he might not be receptive to your Active Listening:

- *Correct me if I'm wrong ...*
- *I think I hear you saying ...*
- *I'm not sure I'm with you ...*
- *Is there any chance that...?*
- *Let me see if I understand you ...*

- *Could this be what's going on ...?*
- *Is it possible that...?*

So when someone comes to you with a strong feeling or a *pickle,* what is the best way for you to initiate Active Listening?

We recommend you use the simple phrase: "Did I hear you say .. ?" It gives you a moment to think and then to feedback the facts and feelings as you think you've heard them. It works like a charm because it allows the children (or person) with the *pickle,* to speak — to be the expert about their problem while you, respectfully, and actively listen.

EXAMPLES:

Child: *I don't want to go to school today.*

Parent: *(feeding back what she thinks she has heard) Did I hear you say you don't want to go to school today?*

Child: *It's book report day, and I remember from last time that standing in front of the class is scary.*

Parent: *(feeding back facts and feelings) Did I hear you say the last time you did your book report in front of the class you were scared?*

Child: *But why does the teacher make us do book reports anyway?*

Parent:	*It sounds like you might be feeling upset that they gave you book reports to do.*
Child:	*Yeah. It's not just the book report, it's standing in front of the class and being laughed at.*
Parent:	*(truly illuminated by all this unexpected information, respectfully continues) So you feel laughed at when you stand up and do your book report? I'd like to hear more about it.*
Child:	*Yeah. They made fun of me last time 'cause I started crying.*
Parent:	*Sounds like that might have hurt your feelings.* Uh huh...
Child:	*Yeah, it did hurt my feelings. When my friends cry I try to make them feel better.*

Do you see what happened? That parent has had a real communication with her son. The mother listened, the child talked. The mother fed-back the child's facts and feelings, and the child offered more information, detailing what was going on for him. Active Listening works! You can bet that the next time that child says, "I don't want to go to school", there's going to be another very real feeling behind the statement. And you can bet his mom will hear all about it because she will Actively Listen rather than give the automatic response: "Of course you're going to school. Now get your shoes on."

This is not to imply that after an Active Listening conversation the child will not be going to school. Sure he will. But not because mom shut him down and told him he had to. He'll go because expressing his feelings is acceptable behavior in the family, but more importantly he'll go feeling better about things because he and mom talked it out.

This may feel slightly odd for you – not to solve the problem, just to listen to it. But that's what we want you to do for now. The reality is when you feedback facts and feelings to someone having a *pickle,* they will feel attended to and cared about. If they are used to you handing them advice and solutions it may take *Cool!* them a while to come to terms with this new system – but remember, it is not your job to fix another's *pickle.* Your job is to help someone with strong feelings express those feelings. And you may very well find after Active Listening, that your child is off and running having felt heard and cared about.

Establishing Active Listening early when our children are babies is a good way to establish this new language with them. In this way, we are acknowledging and attending to our non-verbal child. When the baby cries, we can say, "Oh, are you hungry? Or did you hear a loud noise that frightened you?" This is Active Listening at its best. Your infant can hear your sincerity, your genuineness, and feel your attention. These forms of behavior between parent and child need to continue for a lifetime.

We can and should also pay attention to non-verbal cues. When a toddler is playing happily on a swing, we can say, "I see you are really enjoying swinging on the swing set. I see a big smile on your face!" Or, in another case, "I saw your brother knock you down. I see a frown on your face."

Identifying what you see allows the child to feel seen, heard and valued. Let's continue with a few more conversations in which the parent Active Listens and the child talks. Not all Active Listening conversations go on very long—once the feelings are discharged the conversation generally winds down or the speaker moves on to a different topic.

~~~~~~~~~~~~~~~**EXERCISE**~~~~~~~~~~~~~~~

Use Active Listning responses to each of the following statements:
- No one likes me.
- I need a bigger room.
- Everyone at the party was drinking.
- I can't do anything right.

~~~~~~

EXAMPLES:

I don't want to go to school today. They're giving big tests.

(Yes, The child has a pickle. You Active Listen.)

Dad, will you help me fix my bike?

(The child is simply asking for physical assistance. Answer the question.)

Mom, I don't like it when you keep changing the channels on the TV.

(Yes, The child has feelings about this. You Active Listen.)

Hey, look at this painting I made at school!

(No Active Listening required—just describe what you see.)

Your child comes roaring through the house after school, drops his stuff in the middle of the living room and says "Ugghh..."

(Yes, Active Listen.)

Dad, do you want to play ball after dinner?

(Simple request, Simple response.)

Dad, Annie's father plays ball with us every night after dinner. How come you never do?

(Yes, You Active Listen. Your child has strong feelings here.)

A Sad But True Story

One afternoon many years ago, when my daughter was less than three months old, I was speaking on the phone to a contractor who was interested in helping me re-do my kitchen. At one point in our conversation he politely excused himself, cupped a hand over his phone and proceeded to rant to someone in the room with him, "You stupid idiot. Didn't I tell you ... blah, blah, blah". This man was rude, impolite, and unpleasant and I wondered to whom he was talking. I knew I didn't want to do business with anyone who spoke like that. When he returned to the phone he said, "I was just speaking to my son." I was horrified. It was at that moment that I decided never, ever to speak to my beloved child that way or anyone else for that matter. Toward me, an adult, this man was attentive, polite and interested. With his teen-age son, he was irresponsible, nasty and downright rude.

The sad truth is that many of us don't quite know how to talk to our children. A lot of parents sound just like that contractor.

It's true that children are not adults, so you might feel you can't talk to them exactly like you talk to your friends. But children are also individuals who deserve respect and sensitivity from us.

Our children come through us. They don't belong to us in the same way a painting or table belongs to us. Children are special and unique. Consciously or unconsciously we impress upon them our values and beliefs. But we must also value and honor who they are and how they feel.

HIGHLIGHTS

- Get down to eye level.

- Did I hear you say ... ? Repeat exactly what you've heard.

- Identify a possible feeling.

- Open the door to additional communication.

- Use lead-ins to stimulate further communication.

You have now earned your Learner's Permit

PROVISIONAL INSTRUCTION PERMIT
PERMITS PARENTING ONLY. NOT FOR ID PURPOSES

C4YRSLF   Class A   Issued_____ Expires_____   AL#2PUSE
                                        Date   Date
Certificate of simultaneous enrollment in book study and laboratory phase of Parent Education.

Name _____
Address _____
_____
_____

Sex: (M)/(F) Hair: (YES) (NO) Eyes: (OPEN) (CLOSED)
Patience _____Understanding _____Love_____

I CERTIFY that I am enrolled in book
study phase of Parent Education as
well as in the hands-on Parent Training
in my home. Pursuant to real life, real time,
and in-home Certification.

Signature_____

ALL ACCESS
PICKLE
PASS

Keep reading to qualify for your *"License to Parent"*

103

CHAPTER 6

Recognizing Active Listening

Recognizing Active Listening

~~~~~~

Read through the following responses. Check off the Active Listening response— the response that you feel feeds back what you think you heard.

Child: *I never get to do anything.*

Parent: *A.*   *Of course you get to do things.*

                            B.   *I hear you saying that you feel you never get to do anything. It sounds as if there might be something special that you'd like to do.*

                            C.   *You're never happy.*

Child: *Other kids get to go snow-boarding all the time.*

Parent: *A.*   *Well, you go rollerblading*

                            B.   *It seems as if you might be feeling left out when the other kids go away.*

                            C.   *If you stop whining I'll give you 5 books.*

Child:	*All the kids are going to Charlie's party.*

Parent:	A.	*You're not going.*
	B.	*All kids drink at parties.*
	C.	*Sounds like you'd like to go to Charlie's party.*

Child:	No *one's ever around when I want to play.*

Parent:	A.	*Did I hear you say no one's ever around when you want to play?*
	B.	*Just find other friends to play with.*
	C.	*All you do is complain. Why don't you watch TV?*

Door Openers, Acknowledgements, Non-Verbal Cues

You are probably becoming aware that Active Listening takes time. It does. It deserves time. Ultimately, it will create time for you and your family because you will be communicating directly — less miscommunication, fewer scenes and tantrums. You can do it.

Wow!

What we've been learning about is more than waiting until the other person stops talking so you can say what you want to say. "Listening", we now know, is feeding back facts and

108

feelings. This shows the speaker you respect his unique experiences as he is sharing them.

People often <u>miscommunicate</u>. Sometimes we're not aware of our needs and feelings. Sometimes our emotions interfere with our ability to communicate clearly and respectfully. It's not necessarily anyone's fault, but it happens.

Listen again — with awareness.

Teenager: *I had the worst day at work.*

Dad: *Did I hear you say you had an awful day at work?*

Teenager: *No. I had the WORST day at work.*

Dad: *Wow! You had the WORST day at work. I'd like to hear more about that.*

Notice that the father did not feedback exactly what his son said. His son corrected him and said "No, I had the worst day." The father accepted the correction, and his teenager felt heard.

By feeding back what you think you heard, you will confirm the speaker's facts and feelings or you will indicate to them that you know you need clarification and allow them to bring you up to speed so you can participate in the speaker's reality.

In the situation above, this teenager waited for his dad to repeat his words exactly: "You had the worst day at work." It was the teenager's day so he is the expert. His father's response, while innocent enough, may have sounded to his son as if he were trying to downplay the strength of his emotions, which is not what he needed. The teenager needs to feel heard.

If the speaker corrects you, go with it. Maybe later he will downgrade his day to "awful" but that's up to him, not you.

Uh huh...

The question, "Did I hear you say ... ?" is valuable in that it allows the listener to confirm what we think we heard. And guess what? Sometimes we hear wrong. Feeding back what we think we hear is a responsible way to assure the speaker that we are tracking their story and that we are interested.

Non-Verbal Cues

In addition to oral language, there is also non-oral language. Actively Listen to non-verbal cues. With little children you can feed-back to them what you see.

When a child is happy at play...

Parent: *I see a big smile on your face! Looks like you're having fun on that swing.*

When the child is having a hard time...

Parent: *I see a sad face.*

When a child is happily playing alone in his room (remember, praise can be a wonderful gift if you simply describe what you see)...

Parent: *I see you organizing your toys and putting them away in neat piles!*

When you talk to your children like this, you are helping them grow up to be the people you hope they'll be - and that includes becoming effective communicators for themselves as well as for others.

You are picking up your fifteen-year-old son after a party. When he gets in the car he's silent. But there's an unhappy expression on his face.

Parent: *Looks like you're not feeling too happy.*
Teenager: *Well, the party wasn't that much fun.*

You now look over and notice your child's clothes look different.

Parent: *I see a shirt with the tails out.*
Teenager: *That's the style.*

You see that his new shoes—which cost you a lot of money—look different.

Parent: *I see your shoelaces are gone!*
Teenager: *Yup.*

Now, as far as the teen is concerned, this conversation is over. If you, his parent, are feeling frustrated or mad about those shoes, you now have a *pickle*. Do not try to Active Listen here because the problem is now yours, not your teenager's.

If both you and someone else are in a heated discussion— meaning you both have strong feelings—this also isn't the time for you to try to Active Listen to the other. Your strong feelings will get in the way. Instead, you'll want to be sincere and say, "Since I can't put my feelings aside right now, I cannot effectively Active Listen to you at this time."

Wow!

Sometimes, while Active Listening, we "overshoot" the feelings we think we hear.

Teen: *I hate statistics.*
Parent: *Sounds like you're scared of statistics.*
Teen: *No. I'm not scared. I just hate statistics.*

Okay, you were wrong. You misunderstood. Don't let your ego get in the way here. You don't have to be right. Accept the correction and continue to Active Listen.

Child: *I hate seeing you and my baby sister in a room together.*
Dad: *Did I hear you say you don't like seeing your baby sister and me in a room together?*
Child: *No. I hate seeing you and the baby in a room together.*
Dad: *Did I hear you say you really don't like seeing the baby and me...*
Child: *No! I hate seeing my baby sister and you in a room together.*

The speaker may very well repeat himself until you say the words back to him, and it may be painful for you to hear and to say them – but please repeat exactly what he said to you. Accept his experience. Honor his words.

Child: *I hate seeing you and my baby sister in a room together.*

Dad: *Did I hear you say you hate seeing the baby and me in a room together?*

Child: *Yes.*

Dad: *I'd like to hear more about that.*

Hmmm...

At this point, you can probably tell the child still has very strong feelings, so be descriptive and use the information you have. You may have insight into what this little child is trying to tell you. And if you work together, you may get to the *pickle* behind these feelings.

Just because you Active Listen to your child about his not wanting you to go to work, does not mean that you are not going to work. When children state that they don't want to go to school that doesn't mean that they don't go to school. All of this conversation is taking place while you are getting him dressed for school and while you are getting ready for work.

In such a conversation, you may find that in your role of Active Listener you have a chance to redirect some of the child's attention and focus — but only after the gift of Active Listening has been given.

Here's some more parent/child conversation to scrutinize:

Let's play!

Child: *I hate my little brother.*

Mother: *Did I hear you say you hate your little brother?*

Child: *Yes, I hate him and I want you to give him away.*

Mother: *So you hate him and you want me to give him away? Might you be feeling angry?*

Child: *I'm more than angry, he gets into all my stuff. I hate him and I want him to go away.*

Mother: *So he gets into all your stuff and you think he should go away?*

Child: *He's such a pest and he's always around.*

Mother: *He's always around. He gets into your stuff. He's a pest. Sounds like you're feeling sick of being anywhere near your brother.*

Child: *Exactly. I never get to be alone.*

Mother:	*So, you say you never get to be alone? I'd like to hear more about that.*
Child:	*Sometimes I just want to hit him.*
Mother:	*You just feel so frustrated you want to hit him.*
Child :	*Yeah, but I know people are not for hitting.*

There is a difference between fantasy and reality. Children should be encouraged to speak about their anger. Getting angry feelings out is important. Remember, the job of the parent is to encourage children to express their feelings.

Child:	*I have a stomachache. I can't go to school today.*
Father:	*Did I hear you say you have a stomach ache and can't go to school today?*
Child:	*Yes. My stomach hurts all over.*
Father:	*Wow! Your stomach hurts all over? I'd like to hear more about that.*
Child:	*My stomach hurts because I have too much to do.*
Father:	*Uh-huh...*
Child:	*It hurts all over—from the bottom of my tummy all the way to the top of my shoulders.*

Wow!

Father: *I'd like to hear more about those shoulders of yours...*

Child: *They just feel so heavy.*

Father: (repeating and observing) *So your shoulders are heavy, your stomach is hurting, your thinking is heavy, your eyebrows are smooshed together.*

Child: *I have too much to do and I can't do it all.*

Father: *So I'm hearing you say that doing all you have to do makes your stomach hurt. And you can't do it all?*

Child: *My stomach hurts. I can't do it all. Maybe I can do some of it later.*

Father: *Uh-huh...*

So, as you can see, there are many different, fun and helpful ways to Active Listen. In this case, just Active Listening on the father's part helped the child begin to solve his *pickle*.

We are encouraging you to listen and respond creatively. You can add an air of lightness to the other's situation by first accepting and acknowledging it, then you can have some fun. Respond with levity when appropriate. Respond with love.

A New Spin

A great spin to add to Active Listening is to give your child his fantasy in words. Sometimes it would just be fun to imagine the world in fantasy. It would be fun to fly to the moon on a red horse. It would be fun to have all the ice cream in the world in mounds of chocolate, vanilla and strawberry. And sometimes a fantasy diversion with a touch of Active Listening makes a difficult situation palatable. Here's what we mean...

Child: *Dad, let's get off the freeway. I'm sick of this traffic jam.*

Parent: *Did I hear you say you're sick of this traffic jam? Sounds like you're feeling a little frustrated.*

Child: *Yeah, I'm frustrated and I'm upset. We are supposed to be at the park playing volleyball right now.*

Parent: *So, we should be at the park right now and you're feeling frustrated and upset. I'd like to hear more about that.*

Child: *Well, even when we make a special plan to be together it seems like we spend half the time with you driving and swearing at traffic, and me sitting in the back feeling bored.*

Parent: (injecting fantasy) *Wow! You're sitting back there feeling bored, you hate the traffic, and we're not spending quality time together. If we could get off this next exit where would you want it to be?*

Awesome!

Child: (surprised, delighted) *Anywhere?*

Parent: *Sure. Anywhere. How about if we'd exit and just over that hill would be Hidden Lake where we all camped last summer. Our tent is ready and waiting for us so we don't have to carry it with our packs.*

Child: *Yeah! How about we'd get to ride horses to get to our camp? That way we wouldn't have to carry our packs at all.*

Parent:	*And I'd order one light thunderstorm once we got to our camp-but the storm wouldn't scare the horses or get our food wet. It would just make the place smell wonderful...*

Look what's happening. The child is no longer sullen and bored. It's now a father and son having a fun conversation in the car. The situation and relationship have changed dramatically. It's no longer a father and son stuck in traffic and fuming privately. Communication can be fun! This is why we would choose to give our child his fantasy in words. It's a gift we can all use!

Here's another example...

Child:	*Dad, I want you to stay home with us today.*
Parent:	*Did I hear you say you want me to stay home with you today?*
Child:	*I'd be so much happier if you stayed home from work. It's much more fun when you're home.*
Parent:	(Knowing full well that today he must go to work) *You would like me to stay home so you'll feel happy and we can have fun — maybe rent a dinosaur, go for a ride. What color should our dinosaur be?*
Child:	*Blue! And we can play football and teach our blue dinosaur to kick field goals.*

Parent:	*And we could take the dinosaur to the biggest pool in town.*
Child:	*And when we get thirsty we can empty out the water in the pool and fill it with apricot juice.*
Parent:	*Yeah, and then we can buy the pizza parlor so that for every dinner time we'll just go pick up a free pizza. For dessert we'll teach the pizza people to make chocolate chip/butterscotch pizza!*
Child:	(blown away by the fun in this) *YEAH!*

This Rocks!

Now the truth is — well, you know. You can't rent a dinosaur. This parent won't be buying the pizza parlor, has no access to the biggest pool in town, knows no recipe for chocolate chip/butterscotch pizza — but that's not what's important. What is important is that a conversation took place that was fun, entertaining and interesting. Undoubtedly, the child is feeling pleased, heard and attended to, even though the parent is getting ready to go to work as they're speaking.

Quality Time

~~~~~~

Quality time. It's now. It's today. It's whenever you truly talk and listen to someone you care about. After your child spills his milk and before you put stinging medicine on your son's cut knee — it's now.

The opportunities are all around us. You will begin to carve quality time out of your otherwise busy day by bringing in these new Active Listening skills. Phones interrupt. Friends interrupt. Work interrupts. Life is tricky. But you are now in the process of creating a common language with your family. And, with a common language, your family and loved ones can get through and enjoy so much more of life's challenges. You will learn to talk about all the *pickles*, interruptions and trickiness — even in traffic jams!

Imagine a half-hour or an hour of pure family time at home each evening when the TV is off and the phone is not picked up — a block of time in which members of the family are together and focus on each other. You'll probably find that you and your family talk about all the things that true relationships encompass: teachers, bosses, ups, downs, the weather, the ozone, what's for dinner, what's for dessert, why math is so hard. You can communicate about all the real stuff, especially now that you can offer them your Active Listening behavior. Active Listening is one of the "how-to's" of quality time. It's how you get there and how you stay there.

"Because I'm a kid, That's Why"

An eight-year-old boy was out having dinner with his mother, father and sister. When the milkshake that he ordered arrived he put in the straw, stirred it around, and began drinking. The family was chatting amiably, having a very nice time.

At a certain point the young boy focused his attention on his drink. He realized that if he slurped through the straw and filled his mouth with milk, he could dribble it out of the side of his lips, creating a white mustache and goatee as it dripped down his chin. Thrilled by his own creativity he began to slurp up the milkshake creating his idea in real life. He was having a great time.

Seeing these actions, the boy's father became flustered and started screaming at him, "What are you doing? What's the matter with you? What a mess! Why are you doing that? Why can't you sit at the table and drink your milkshake like a regular person? What's wrong with you? Why? Why? Why??!!"

His son replied, "Because I'm a kid, that's why."

Suddenly, the father was amused by his son's remark. He felt embarrassed by his own reaction. At that moment he was able to say, "You're right, son, you are a kid. I apologize. You're only eight-years-old. Decorating yourself with milkshake probably seemed like fun. However, in a restaurant, having milk come out of your mouth is inappropriate. Can you find another way to be an eight-year old? And the family continued their good time at dinner.

HIGHLIGHTS

• Listen for door openers.

• Conversation is on a lot of topics.

• Communication is on one topic.

• Look for non-verbal cues.

• Just because you Active Listen to your child not wanting you to go to work does NOT mean you don't go to work.

• Have fun fun fun!

Obstacles to Communication
Boundaries and Rules

Boundaries and Rules of Behavior

Boundaries are behavioral lines that can be moved.
Rules are behavioral lines that cannot be moved.
A rule is an absolute. It cannot be changed. No hitting is a rule. When this behavior takes place there must be a direct and consistent consequence. If a child engages in hitting behavior that child will get an age-appropriate consequence. For example, a 5-year-old may be sent to his room, or a 10-year-old may be sent to his room, asked to write a letter of apology or given an extra chore. Naturally, the parent will Active Listen to the child's feelings and then follow through with the appropriate consequence.

Parents must learn to accept feelings and encourage the expression of such needs and feelings while providing boundaries and rules about acceptable and unacceptable behavior.

Rules:

Children do not play with butcher knives.

No playing in the street.

People are not for biting.

Boundaries:

Bedtime is eight o'clock.

No sleepovers on school nights.

Homework gets done before playtime.

Wow!

You, the parent, determine when and how a boundary may be moved.

Example: The TV boundary: No TV during the week!

Your child comes home and tells you that there is a special show on Wednesday at 7:00 pm that he'd like to watch. You both determine that in order to move the boundary he must complete his chores and be responsible for getting his homework done before the show. Furthermore, he must be up and ready to go to school promptly on Thursday morning. Boundaries can move when you and your child and communicate responsibly.

List three boundaries in your family that can occasionally be moved:

_____

_____

_____

List three rules in your family that can never be changed:

_____

_____

_____

A good time to talk about a boundary that's been a problem in the past is when you're in the *no-pickle zone*. When someone has a *pickle* about a boundary, it is not a reasonable time to discuss the subject. Pick a time for discussion when there are no feelings about the issue. For instance, dinnertime is a good time to talk about bedtime.

Children need boundaries. Staying up all night is unacceptable behavior, therefore a boundary is required. A tantrum is an indirect cry for a boundary. If you don't create boundaries for them, children will behave in such a way that puts you in a position where appropriate boundaries must be created. By communicating and staying true to boundaries, you are keeping your word. You are demonstrating your trustworthiness. Children need this.

Great!

State boundaries in factual, non-threatening ways. Just as you say, "Toys belong in the toy chest," say "Bedtime is eight o'clock'" and mean it.

Boundaries need to be firm. Of course, for a special occasion you can change a boundary. But in ordinary cases, keep bedtime (or whatever the boundary) the same.

Keep your word. If you say bedtime is eight o'clock, then bedtime is eight o'clock. Have fun going to bed. Play the "going to bed" game. Children learn more from games and playing than any other manner. "Going to bed" games can be stories, songs, making up rhymes – anything that's enjoyable for you and your child. Remember, one of the reasons you had children is to play with them.

Talk to your children. Haven't we all seen a child coloring happily, and a parent walks up and says, "Come on. We're going to be late for your dentist appointment." The parent whisks them away. Isn't that a bit disrespectful? The child was busy, involved with his life, and suddenly it is all changed.

Be considerate and give him a boundary: "Gee, I see you're really working hard. In a few minutes we will need to get ready to go to the dentist..."

> *...after you finish that yellow line.*
>
> *...in five more minutes.*
>
> *...here's the timer.*
>
> *...after one more thick line.*

Awesome!

These are all boundaries. Boundaries, while serious, can be fun and creative — and occasionally they can also change. Yes! You can change your mind and say: "Wow! We have time for you to do an extra thick line." "Oh, you want to do two more? Next time."

Obstacles to Communication

When parents have small children they often inadvertently create communication obstacles. A communication obstacle gets in the way of communication. Now, the ideal relationship for a parent to have with a child is a relationship in which the child can communicate his feelings, his embarrassments, his shame, his happiness, his frustrations. This is really what you want. You want open, honest, loving communication where you don't necessarily have to agree with what your child is saying, but you give him respect and space to have his own opinions and feelings.

Here are some ways in which parents block the flow of communication between the parent and the child. We have attached labels so you can identify your communication style. See it, hear it, alter it. Are you ... ?

The Contoller   The Caretaker

The Judge   The Detective

The Controller

Being the controller is a big communication barrier. If you have to be in control, what you're doing is *providing solutions*. Your child doesn't learn to work things out for himself. People in control have the need to be right, which causes someone else to feel wrong. The child of a controller often feels insecure and frightened of life. Sometimes, they strike out in an effort to feel free.

The controller says:

- *You can never do anything right.*
- *I know better than you.*
- *Do it now or else.*

The Judge

The Judge *finds fault and ridicules.* This forces your child to stuff his true feelings, possibly forever. The Judge makes children feel as if they can't do anything right. Children feel ridiculous, stupid, and blamed for having their opinions and feelings. Unfortunately, when you judge children they feel as if something is wrong with them. And that affects their self-worth. It makes them feel bad about themselves. And it takes away their own sense of responsibility. When your child comes downstairs dressed for school wearing a yellow shirt, blue pants, green socks, orange shoes, and a purple belt...

The Judge says:

- *Go back to your room and put on matching clothes.*
- *Oh! That's great. Do you want me to be the laughing stock of the school?*
- *You look silly.*

Ahhh!

133

The Caretaker

The Caretaker creates an obstacle to communication by *minimizing the importance of the situation.* This obstacle is sneaky and hard to spot because it sounds as if the Caretaker is soothing and concerned. Caretakers praise. They agree. They reassure. They sympathize. But they also trivialize the other's experience.

The Caretaker says:

- *Don't worry, it's not important.*
- *Let's talk about other things.*
- *There, there, it's always darkest just before the dawn.*

When your teenager comes home and says, "I can't pay for my gas", and you say, "Don't worry", would that response be comforting to you?

If your child comes home and says, "Will I know anybody at camp?" and you respond with, "Ah, things will work out," will that help him in this moment?

What happens is that this kind of message from the Caretaker denigrates the importance of the situation and may evoke expectations that everything will get better soon. Caretakers negate the magnitude of the experience by denying its difficulty. Caretakers can be well intentioned. They might think that making light of a situation will bring relief. But, children need to feel and come to terms with their own hurts and fears. The experience must be experienced.

The Detective

Then there's the Detective. What Detectives do is *analyze, explain, diagnose and even argue.*

The Detective says:

• *When did you lose your shoes?*

• *What happened to the new shirt I bought?*

• *Who did you hang out with at the party?*

• *Why were you late?*

• *Where did you go?*

• *Who did you go with and when?*

This kind of intrusive probing provokes a defensive position and creates the need to fight with, or flee from, the inquisitor. It feels invasive. It provokes a need for self-protection and it creates a desire in the child to disappear.

What you've done is to act like the District Attorney. Your child's heart starts pounding and he gets scared. Is that what you want — your child to feel scared? You may not agree with what is going on, but if you want to leave the communication obstacles out of your relationship you have to open up the space for communication to flow.

The Professional Parent

Parents don't have to agree with what their children say. However, it has to be okay for children to have an opening for expression. What you want to do is take the obstacles of communication out of the picture and replace them with a safe place where your child's opinion and feelings are listened to and respected. You want to keep the lines of communication open so that there's a flowing dialogue between you and your child.

The way to have an informative, pleasing dialogue between parent and child is by using Active Listening, door openers and the language of feelings. The professional parent helps the other *Great!* person to identify what they might be feeling, describes what they see, listens with attention and shows respect to the person who is talking.

The professional parent says...

- *Did I hear you say...?*

- *So you think that would be the best choice for you...?*

- *I'd like to hear more about it...*

136

Graduate School

~~~~~~

Cydney tells this story about her dad:

When it was time for me to go to graduate school I applied to a particular one in Los Angeles. The admissions office at the school told me that only very few of the many applicants would be accepted. The odds seemed overwhelming. When I told my father the story he responded as a **caretaker**, "Don't worry, you'll get in." I became furious and in that moment needed to express how much I hated his response. What happened? What went wrong?

By ignoring my feelings and predicting a future that he could not have possibly foreseen my dad closed down the conversation that might have been. I was afraid of not getting into this school because so few applicants were accepted. I was feeling insecure because it seemed that the odds were against me. My dad was trying to make me feel better, but by not attending to what was really going on inside me he made matters worse.

My dad had created an obstacle to communication. The pressure was increased, not lessened. I felt inadequate and stupid. His intention, of course, was to take away my scared feelings. What if I didn't make it? Would he be disappointed? Lose faith in me? Would I let him down?

It seemed my dad was really trying to make himself feel better when he said, "Don't worry, you'll get in. You're a good student." I worried even more. Instead of dealing with my nervousness he ignored it. The words, "Don't worry" did not make me "not worry". Those words created even more anxiety.

What communication would have hit the mark? I would have felt better if he had responded, "It sounds as if you're concerned that you might not get into this school because so few people are accepted every year."

HIGHLIGHTS

- Boundaries are behavioral lines that can move.

- Rules are behavioral lines than cannot move.

Are You?
- The Controller
- The Judge
- The Caretaker
- The Detective
- The Professional Parent

- A Professional Parent avoids obstacles to communication.

CHAPTER 8

Talk So Your Children
Will Hear You

Talk So Your Children
Will Hear You

Along with Active Listening, here is another set of skills that will change your life for the better. This other important set of skills is called *My-messages*. My-messages are used either when there is NO *pickle* and you have something to say, or YOU have the *pickle*. The My-message belongs to "me". It is "my" problem. It is "my" *pickle*. It is "my" upsetness. Therefore, in order to dispel my problem, I must give my message to the person who is involved.

Sending Direct Messages

The responsible communicator:

- Heads off problems by sending positive, non-threatening messages whenever possible.

- Recognizes and is responsible for his own feelings and needs.

- Pays attention, listens to others and sets a climate for receptivity.

Hmmm...

- Allows for interaction and discussion.

- Knows the difference between aggressive (demanding) and assertive (asking/stating) behavior.

My-messages

~~~~~~

My-messages are about *me,* the speaker. This is a message that I want to convey to you, the listener. My-messages do not include the word **"YOU."** That's because often the word "you" makes the person who is listening feel defensive. It also can make the person who is listening feel as if they are being told what to do. My-messages are all about the person who is speaking, because the person doing the speaking has information to convey. That's *me* wanting to convey a message to *you.*

This type of communication expresses needs and feelings, both positive and negative, about behavior. My-messages identify behavior, express a feeling, communicate a need, and, in some cases, describe a concrete reaction or response to the other person. A My-message eliminates the <u>negative</u> "you." A My-message, delivered correctly, does not provoke a defensive response. Negative "You-messages" cause people to feel defensive and it's hard to listen when you're busy defending yourself.

Negative "you-messages" blame and accuse: Wow!

Negative you-message: *You're never on time.*

Positive my-message:	*I feel frustrated when my movie partner doesn't arrive on time.*
Negative you-message:	*You're so selfish.*
Positive my-message:	*I feel discounted when my needs aren't being considered.*

My-messages involve self-disclosure. They are often a communication about your personal beliefs, ideas, likes, dislikes, feelings, thoughts and reactions.

Possible my-messages when you're in the NO PICKLE zone

These are three types of my-messages:

- Accepting my-message
- Informative my-message
- Preventive my-message

Accepting *my-messages* strengthen the relationship by sharing positive feelings.

- *When I see how neat and organized the closet is, I feel relieved because now I can find things.*
- *When I hear a sister and brother talking quietly and sharing books, it makes my heart feel big and happy.*

145

Informative *my-messages* let the other know what you're thinking.

• *I love you.*

Preventive *my-messages* let others know of a future need you will have, and provide the other with the opportunity to cooperate.

• *Tomorrow I need to use the TV and the VCR at 8:00 pm. There is a show I must tape for the class I am teaching.*

• *In the next few days I would like to make time for the two of us to visit my mother.*

Possible my-messages when you're in the Pickle Zone

Yes, it's true. Sometimes the *pickle* **is** your *pickle*. And that puts you in the *Pickle* Zone. Here's how you deal with it. If **I** have a *pickle* that's a reason to use a my-message. When the message you want to communicate is "this behavior does not work for me" then **you** have the *pickle*. A My-message will help you convey this information.

My-messages are a non-punitive way of describing unacceptable behavior, your feelings about that behavior, and its consequences for you. My-messages are complex because they include:

146

- *Identifying the behavior*
- *Your feelings*
- *The effect this behavior may have on you*
- *Consequences.*

Here's how it works:

Step 1: Identify the behavior that you see or hear. Be as specific as you can by saying: "When I see..." or "When I hear..."

When I see dirty dishes in a sink that I have just cleaned up before going to work ...

When I hear loud screaming while I'm having people over...

Step 2: Identify a feeling. Be as specific as you can:

... I feel angry and not cared about...

Wow!

... I feel frightened

Step 3: Identify an effect that the unwanted behavior may have caused you. Be as specific as you can:

...and it will take me extra time to clean up the kitchen, so dinner will be late.

...and it takes me away from my guests and having fun.

Step 4: You may also add a consequence that the behavior has provoked:

...and it will not leave enough time to go to the movies tonight.

...and it causes me to want to stop offering my chauffeuring service.

Now, put these responses all together into a compound my-message:

When I see dirty dishes in the sink after I have just cleaned up before going to work, I feel angry and not cared about. It will take me extra time to clean up the kitchen, so dinner will be late, and it will not leave enough time to go to the movies tonight.

When I hear loud screaming while I'm having people over, I feel concerned. It takes me away from my guests and having fun, and it causes me to want to stop offering my chauffeuring service.

Notice how this communication does not use the word "you" or point a finger at the other. It simply addresses how "I" feel about the issue, its effect, and what the consequences will be.

Step 1: Identify the unacceptable behavior.

Step 2: Articulate your feeling.

Step 3: Specify what effect the behavior has on you.

Step 4: When appropriate, communicate the consequences of the behavior.

Identify the unacceptable behavior first so the listener knows exactly what you're talking about. The more descriptive you are, the better the listener can understand and attempt to fulfill your needs. Specific descriptions work.

Rather than saying, *"Who threw the towels in the bathroom?"*

Say, *"When I see dirty towels thrown all over the bathroom and a dirty tub..."*

Rather than saying, *"Stop the screaming!"*

Say, *"When I hear a brother and a sister screaming so loudly, I can't think and I feel helpless."*

Rather than saying, *"What have you got to complain about?"*

Say, *"When I hear crying over a new birthday present..."*

When you describe behavior, you ensure that your child recognizes what you're talking about and this engages him. He must be able to identify his unacceptable behavior before he can deliberately change it.

When you describe your feelings the child will know how the behavior has made you feel.

When you offer the effect the behavior has on you, the listener can see how you both may be affected by this behavior.

When you communicate the consequence of the behavior, the child will know how his behavior has ultimately affected *him*.

- *When I see hitting behavior I feel upset, and it causes me to want to change plans about going to the park.* Communication doesn't get much clearer than this!

Speaking with my-messages puts your energy in a positive place rather than in a negative place (making judgments, holding grudges, threatening or acting out behaviors).

Let's discuss the effects of behavior for a minute: When you see new white shoes in puddles, how might this effect you?

Hmmm...

- *I hate it when the shoes get dirty.*
- *If I have to clean them, this will take time.*
- *If I have to replace them, this will cost money and time.*

When you have just spent three hours cooking a gourmet dinner for your family, and your family doesn't offer to help with the dishes – what could be an effect?

- *It causes me not to want to cook for the family.*

When you describe behavior and share its effects and consequences with your children it helps them understand that you are mad at their behavior, not at them. Behavior can change. You are upset with the behavior — children are not their behavior.

- *When I hear whining for strawberry milk I feel upset, and it causes me to want to leave the room.*

• *When I see the lights left on in my bathroom I feel unheard. And, because I'm concerned about wasting energy, it makes me not want to have the television on.*

Be specific.

Rather than saying, *"Stop that!"*
Say, *"When I see pulling on toys, grabbing and pushing."*

This way children know exactly what you are talking about. Use a MY-message:

• *When I see pulling on toys, grabbing and pushing, I feel cheated because I know this could be a fun family time and it causes me to want to be alone.*

Go for clarity. Keep it simple. Start with the behavior you don't like. Limit your choice of emotions to one. Be specific. This helps your listener stay focused. Avoid the use of the word "YOU".

• *When I hear whining and see foot-stamping behavior when we're in the supermarket, I feel unappreciated, and it causes me to not want to go to the toy store.*

Ah ha!

When you give your message, you might get a defensive response. So deliver your responsible my-message again.

My-message:

• *When I come home from a trip and the dog isn't fed and the cat isn't groomed, and there's doggie water all over the floor, I feel so frustrated that it causes me to think about withholding the present I brought.*

151

The other person may now be experiencing a problem and you need to listen to them. Shift gears to Active Listen to their response.

Response, *"But, unexpectedly, I had to work twelve hours yesterday..."*

You can then Active Listen and restate your original or modified my-message as the dialogue continues:

• *Did I hear you say that you unexpectedly had to work twelve hours yesterday? Still, when I come home from a trip and the dog isn't fed and the cat isn't groomed, and there's doggie water all over the floor, I feel so frustrated it causes me to think about withholding the present I brought.*

Learning how to construct these responsible sentences is simple, but it's not easy. In the beginning phases of crafting my-messages it might help you to write them out first. Give yourself a moment before you respond to the situation and think things through so that your communication will be responsible and effective. Jot down the unacceptable behavior, your feelings, the effect it has on you and the consequences. That way, you are sure you're my-message is short, specific and does not include the word "you."

Here's your *pickle.*

You come home to find your living room is covered in pizza and soda cans. There is a half-eaten pizza on the white carpet. You have a school meeting at your house in 40 minutes. Resist the urge to throttle, spank, yell, and cry. Go through the mental list of Behavior, Feeling, Effect, Consequence and craft a responsible my-message.

~~~~~~~~~~~~~~~~~**EXERCISE**~~~~~~~~~~~~~~~~~

Create a My-message to this situation in your own words:

When I see_____I

feel_____

it causes me _____.

~~~~~~

Does your exercise sound something like this?

<u>When I see</u> pizza all over the table and chairs <u>I feel</u> frustrated because I have a lot of people coming here tonight, and <u>it causes me</u> to want to ban hanging out in the living room.

Your teen may respond to your my-message with:

But I didn't mean to. Besides all my friends were here. What was I supposed to do?

A little Active Listening shift to the teen's point of view...

Parent: *Did I hear you say all your friends were here and you didn't know what to do? Maybe you felt that doing something would be embarrassing.*

Teen: *Yes. Telling everybody not to hang out would have been really embarrassing.*

(Return to original my-message because your *pickle* is still your pickle)

Parent: *When I see messy pizza all over the table and chairs I feel frustrated because I have a lot of people coming here tonight, and it causes me to want to ban hanging out.*

Teen: *I don't do this all the time. I don't think you should blame me.*

This Rocks!

(Shift to Active Listening)

Parent: *So you don't want to be blamed. Okay. You may feel like you are a responsible person but I still have people coming tonight for a meeting and look at the room.*

After the my-message was delivered and the Active Listening is offered, the parent and the teen begin to clean up the living room together.

Create a few My-messages:

1._____

_____

_____

_____

_____

_____

2._____

_____

_____

_____

_____

_____

3._____

_____

_____

_____

_____

4._____

_____

_____

_____

_____

Cyrano

~~~~~~

When Cydney was little, about 6-years-old, I used to read wonderful stories to her at night. Some of the stories we read were "Curious George", "Good Night Moon", "Cyrano De Bergerac", "The Velveteen Rabbit", and "Romeo and Juliet". We shared all these wonderful classics.

One day she and I went to a party together. At that time I owned an antique store in Los Angeles and was putting myself through school. I had two people working for me — a husband and a wife. They were also at this party. Trying to be nice to the boss's child, they chatted with my daughter while I was engaged with someone else.

I heard muffled shrieks of laughter coming from the other side of the room. My two associates came bounding toward me to tell their story. Grinning from ear to ear, they began...

They said that they had asked Cydney what kind of stories she liked. Before she could open her mouth to answer they continued, "Do you know the tale of the guy with the long nose?" And she said, "Of course."

They continued, "Do you remember his name?" ...thinking she'd answer Pinocchio.

My daughter responded brightly, "Of course. It was Cyrano!"

The moral of this story is, "Don't talk down to children." Get down with them. They may know more than you think.

HIGHLIGHTS

- My-messages contain information I want to convey to you.

- My-messages do not contain the word "You".

- My-messages identify behavior.

- My-messages explain the feelings about the behavior.

- My-messages describe the effect this behavior has on you.

- My-messages convey responsible consequences.

When a Pickle is Really a Problem

When a Pickle is Really a Problem

As we've discovered in previous chapters, *pickles* can usually be resolved by using the tools of Active Listening and My-messages. However, sometimes a *pickle* is so big and far-reaching (often involving the whole family), that it is definitely a problem. What to do?

Luckily, problem-solving is a very effective technique. This problem-solving technique is the most efficient way of resolution when there is a real issue in your family that needs mediation, clarification or expression.

Problem-solving is a method that takes a good deal of time and effort on everyone's part. It is not a quick-fix. It may be necessary to call a family conference. Everyone involved needs to sit down and spend the time and effort required to resolve the issue.

A Difference of Opinion vs. a Problem

A difference of opinion does not necessarily require a solution. In many cases we can simply agree to disagree. A difference of opinion becomes a problem when *Wow!* it recurs without resolution and interferes with the smooth running of the family. A difference of opinion becomes a problem when the outcome or resolution will have a large or permanent effect on all parties.

Here is an example of a difference of opinion:

Your teenager and you have differing opinions about the relative value of shoelaces in shoes. Are they necessary? Are they cool? You disagree about the need for shoelaces. The teen will talk about style. The parent will talk about tripping and shoes falling off. No agreement is necessary because ultimately the issue doesn't affect the on-going relationship. Shoelaces are good topics for discussion but it isn't necessary to resolve into agreement through problem-solving.

Pick your battles! In the grand scheme of things, shoelaces are small potatoes. Well, actually, they're really just small shoelaces, but you know what we mean. Save the big effort on conflict resolution for the big issues.

Here is an example of a difference of opinion that has the potential to turn into a problem:

Your teen has an after-school job. He has an old, unreliable car that frequently breaks down on his way to work. He is constantly complaining to you about how much he hates to be late for work because he has car trouble. He feels embarrassed, and brings these feelings to you almost daily. It might sound like this:

I hate my car. I never get to work on time.

When you find that this sort of complaining goes on day after day, this is the clue that problem-solving is necessary.

A difference of opinion becomes a problem when it begins to affect more than one person. When your child dyes his hair red that is a difference of opinion. It only becomes a problem if Dad is the president of the bank and worried about his public image, or if Dad is a highly religious person, or mom hates red heads. Then the problem-solving technique will be invaluable for everyone because the **essence of the technique is to communicate until there is a mutually satisfying resolution.** In other words, what we are going to learn is how to solve problems so everyone wins and the relationship thrives.

Obstacles to Solving Problems

When a child comes to you expressing a need or a feeling, do you immediately begin figuring out a solution? Do you stop listening to what they are actually saying and begin to solve what you assume is the problem? Maybe you don't even hear the entire issue because you're in your own head. Many parents think it's their job to solve every problem and untangle each emotional puzzle for their children ("Here, let me fix that for you.").

Unfortunately, taking care of children's problems for them only makes it harder for them to learn to become independent people. Did you ever problem-solve with your parents when you were young? They probably solved your problems for you by telling you what to do. That's what may have been demonstrated when you were a child so, of course, you thought you were supposed to do the same for your own children. But, stop for a moment. Look inside. Did you like it? Nope!

Yeah!

When you solve a problem for a child, you deprive him of learning how to make his own decisions. When a child expresses a need or a feeling, it's often a parental habit to offer solutions. It looks like we're being good parents by helping our children. Right? Wrong. By rushing in to fix things, it's possible that you stop listening, create an obstacle to communication, and begin to solve the problem yourself.

Solving problems with your child invites him to participate with you in finding solutions. It shows him that you value his input. It also shows him that you are aware of how important the problem is to him, and that you will make an effort to work with him on the solution.

Here are the steps to problem-solving so everyone wins:

1. Select a specific time and location to have the discussion.

2. Give each brainstorming participant paper and pencils.

3. Identify the problem using Active Listening and my-messages.

4. Brainstorm some alternative solutions to the problem.

5. Evaluate choices.

6. Choose the solution.

7. Implement the solution.

8. Evaluate how things are going.

Remember the teen whose car wasn't getting him to work on time? Let's use him as an example. We're going to use Active Listening to help our teen identify what might be going on.

The purpose of problem-solving is to find a solution that is genuinely acceptable to all parties involved through fairness, respect and mutual satisfaction.

Setting the Stage: Identify the problem and tell the other that you want to find a win/win situation. Gain the other's willingness before you begin. This procedure can take a lot of time, so create an atmosphere where the participants can work together without distraction. Supply everyone with paper and pencils. Be prepared to devote the quantity and quality of time necessary to reach the conclusion you hope for.

Teen: *I need a new car.*

Dad: *Did I hear you say you need a new car?*

Teen: *I need a new, reliable car.*

Dad: *I hear you say you need a new, reliable car. I'd like to hear more about that.*

Teen: *I'm sick of using a car that doesn't run half the time.*
I'm sick of being late for work and apologizing to my boss.

Dad: *Sounds like you're feeling anxious*

Teen: *Yes, I am anxious and angry. And embarrassed, too.*
I don't like being late and unreliable.

Dad: *So your old car is letting you down and it's*
frustrating.

Teen: *Yeah. I like this job I have. I don't want to lose it*
because I can't show up on time due to my car.

The teen thinks the solution to his problem is a new car. However, his actual needs are independence, control and reliability.

Let's revisit the "I need a new car" scenario. Your teen's solution to the problem is a new car for him. You, as the parent, have already decided and discussed with him that there is no money for a new car. What other solutions might there be to fulfill the actual needs? Here's where you both get creative:

You have determined together that your teen's real needs (therefore, his real problems) are: money, independence, self-assurance, control and reliability.

Brainstorm all solutions you two can think of... silly, funny, straightforward ones. Everything goes on the list; it doesn't have to make sense. Ready? Go.

- Buy a used car
- Fix the old car
- Carpool
- Parent takes teen to work
- Bus
- Bike
- Motorcycle
- Rollerblades
- Train
- Take out a loan
- Share a taxi with a friend
- Find a different job closer to home
- Hitchhike
- Buy a new car

Wow!

After doing some research, you come together again and discuss each option. If your teen says a used car would be acceptable as long as it's reliable, add that amendment to the list. If an option doesn't work, scratch it off the list. Keep going.

- Buy a used car .. must be reliable

- Fix old car .. Scratched off list- mechanic says old car is on its last legs

- Carpool ... an option both teen and parent agree on if the carpool driver is reliable

- Parent takes teen ... scratched off list- not acceptable with teen

- Bus ... an option if the bus route times are *convenient*

- Motorcycle ... scratched off list - not acceptable for parent

- Rollerblades ... scratched off - too far

- Bike ... *if a safe route is found*

- Train ... scratched off - not available

- Take out a loan ... *a possibility*

- Share a taxi with a friend ... scratched off - too expensive

- Find a different job closer to home ... scratched off - not acceptable with teen

- Hitchhike ... scratch off - not acceptable to either

- Buy a new car .. if parent and teen split the cost

Now, as you can tell, this process takes some time. But that is communicating. It does take time, but the payoff is huge. You are not making some decision and handing it down to your child. You and your child work together so no one feels like the loser in the deal.

The second list of acceptable options now looks like this:
- A used car .. must be reliable

- Carpool... an option agreed to by both teen and parent

- Bus ... an option if the bus route times are convenient

- Bike ... if a safe route is found

• Take out a loan ... a possibility

• A new car … if parent and teen split the cost

Remember, agreeing to disagree is imperative in any relationship. However, to get a problem solved, disagreeing is just a step in the direction of finding a mutually acceptable solution. So teen and dad's third list of possibilities looks like this after more research:

• A used car ... must be reliable and must be under $3,000, teen and parents will split the cost

• Carpool ...teen is willing to be in a carpool

• Bus ... scratched - too far, too long for teen

• Bike ... scratched - no safe route is found

• Take out a loan ... scratched - not an option

• A new car … scratched... neither has the money

Choose the solution. Go over the list of remaining options together. Suddenly, with the amendments, getting a used car looks like an acceptable option for both parties.

Implement the solution. Take action. Begin shopping for a used car, the cost of which teen and dad will split. The price limit has been predetermined, and teen will initiate a carpool to keep costs down.

They decide on the adorable red car that has a reliable rebuilt engine and costs under $3,000.

Evaluate the solution after the first week. Is teen getting to work on time? Is the car reliable? Is the carpool working out? Make sure the dates for ten of teen's installment payments to dad are marked on the family calendar and stick to the schedule. Have we solved the problem? Looks good to me!

Here's another example:

Your 6-year-old son shares his bedroom with his 10-year-old brother. He has been complaining about this issue for weeks and is really unhappy. Here's what you do...

Son:	*I need my own room.*
Mother:	*Did I hear you say you need your own room?*
Son:	*Yes, I need a big, new room for myself.*
Mother:	*So, you need a big, new room for yourself. I'd like to hear more.*
Son:	*Now I have to share my room with my big brother and I don't have enough space in my drawers and closet for all my stuff. And I don't have any privacy. So, I need my own room.*
Mother:	*Let me see. You don't have any privacy or space for your stuff.*
Son:	*Yes.*
Mother:	*It sounds as if you may be feeling frustrated at having to share your space and privacy with your brother.*
Son:	*Right! I'm really mad. That's why I need my own room.*

The son thinks the solution to his problem is his own room.

However his actual needs are privacy and space for his stuff.

Step 1: You have concluded what your son's actual needs are by decoding his "I need my own room" coded message. You have Active Listened and are about to implement the problem-solving techniques during a time you two have set aside for a brainstorming session.

Step 2: Brainstorm a list of all the funny, practical and whimsical possible solutions

- Build a bigger closet

- Send big brother away to live with grandma

- Take out the bathroom and make it a playroom just for son

- Build floor-to-ceiling shelves for toys

- Burn all of big brother's stuff in a backyard bonfire

- Throw away all of son's stuff

- Get your son a larger chest of drawers

- Put up a small tent in the corner of the room for privacy

- Buy a new house

Step 3: Talk about each option. Scratch off the ones that simply won't work, and offer amendments to those that are still possible.

- A bigger closet can't be built, but building a closet conversion with double hanging doors and more shelf space is a good idea.

- Grandma will probably not agree to take big brother ... *scratched* off.

- Taking out the bathroom would raise some personal hygiene issues ... *scratched* off.

- Building tall shelves is a distinct possibility.

- Burning big brother's possessions is an unrealizable fantasy ... *scratched* off.

- Throwing away all of your son's stuff is unacceptable to him ... *scratched* off.

- Getting your son a larger chest of drawers is another possibility.

- Putting up a private tent is do-able.

- Buying a new house is not acceptable to you ... *scratched* off.

Now you have some concrete ideas to work with. The second list of possible solutions looks like this:

- Do a closet conversion with all kinds of space-enlarging features—might be rather expensive.

- Build floor-to-ceiling shelves - kits are available at the local home-improvement depot.

- Get a larger chest of drawers - *might be able to find one at a garage sale and paint it whatever color the child wants.*

Step 4. Choose the solution. Everyone agrees that floor-to ceiling shelves would be terrific, and setting up a tent will give him his own, private space. Also, everyone in the family will keep their eyes open for neighborhood garage sales where they might find a large chest of drawers.

Step 5: Implement the solution. Go out to the home improvement depot and buy and install those shelves. Make it a family project. Find a tent that is just the perfect size to fit in a corner of the boys' room. Start checking out garage sales.

Step 6: Evaluate the solution after a short period. Did the shelves provide enough space for his stuff? Is he using his tent? Has his complaining stopped?

Problem-solving techniques work. More than that, they offer an opportunity for family members to work **together** to find a solution. The child feels validated because the parent has put aside special time and effort to help him. He also feels competent and self-reliant because he has contributed to solving the problem. He is important. He can think of good *Right on!* ideas. He is not a victim of his parent's authority. When you give your children the chance to participate in their emotional growth, you help them to feel self-confident and secure in their social interactions.

What Parents Do

We all want our children to be whole, perfect and magnificent.

~~~~~~

"What do you want a boy or a girl?" expectant parents are often asked about their unborn child. They usually respond, "We really don't care as long as it's healthy."

We hope. We hope.

Sometimes our wishes are not granted. Children may be born with life-threatening issues. Some develop problems as they grow. Not all children are born whole and perfect. New parents must learn how to deal with the differences -- the other-ness of their special-needs child.

No parent is ever prepared to handle, understand or cope with a child who comes into this world with a life-threatening disorder, a chronic disease, allergies, asthma, a physical or mental handicap or any other difference. But it happens.

What's a parent to do?

"Professional" parents become students of the differences. They seek out the help of health care providers. They research the issues and problems morning, noon and night. They attend seminars. They bond and share with others whose children are "different". They become their child's advocate. And they advocate for those of others.

It never stops.

The issues change and are layered on top of other issues depending on the child's place in the family, but it never stops.

On a personal note, I observe my daughter and my son-in-law learning how to make the world safe for their sons who came into this world with life-threatening allergies. I watch with wonder and respect as these parents teach their children how to cope with their personal differences -- how they talk about their children's special needs with them. The family focuses on life-saving thoughts and practices about living with allergies.

This father and mother teach their children about what they can safely eat. They educate and discuss the consequences of ingesting food that is harmful to their digestive systems. Their children have to know what they are eating, including the ingredients written in small type. These boys have learned the mantra, "If I can't read the ingredients I can't eat the ingredients." They are discovering. They are learning to manage themselves. Ultimately they will gain the wisdom and knowledge to rely on and TRUST themselves.

I notice the playful games around the dining room table: Mother jokingly role plays, "Do you want my cheese pizza? Yum, Yum!"

"No, I'm allergic", the boys proudly answer. Knowing that answer and being able to express it is important to their lives, health and happiness.

At another time I see and hear their little boy cry, "Why can't I have that? I'm very, very, very SAD." I watch as these parents show empathy for their child's cry. There is no punishment for his expression of feeling. They listen. They lovingly show him more and more about himself and the power he has over his own life.

I observe these parents consciously and consistently providing life-saving information to their children. I watch in awe, admiration and affection.

Cydney and Kenneth, thank you for teaching my grandchildren and me how to navigate independently in this world, to be original thinkers, to feel okay about difference, and to TRUST.

HIGHLIGHTS

- A difference of opinion doesn't require resolution.

- A problem arises when the outcome will affect several people.

- Pick your battles. Use problem-solving techniques where they really matter.

- Don't solve your children's problems for them. Teach them how.

Problem-solving steps:
- Select a specific time and quiet location to have the discussion.
- Give each brainstorming participant paper and pencils.
- Identify the problem using Active Listening and My-Messages.
- Brainstorm some alternative solutions to the problem.
- Evaluate alternatives.
- Choose the solution.
- Implement the solution.
- Evaluate how things are going.

Definitions

~~~~~~

Acceptance: allowing people the right to their own feelings. It builds self-esteem, communicates trust, and creates self-respect in the one who is feeling accepted.

Agreement: a pact between people.

Judgment: an opinion, conclusion or decision about something.

Behavior: the action which can be photographed or recorded.

Character: the personality, individuality, ego, nature, ethical traits and essential quality of the self.

Acceptable behavior: a physical or verbal act that demonstrates support, love, trust and appreciation for others.

Unacceptable behavior: a physical or verbal act that demonstrates disrespect, distrust and a lack of appreciation for others.

The difference between feelings and thoughts:
A _thought_ is a concept, an idea, a notion or a whim. It is brainwork. A _feeling_ is awareness, a sensation. It is bodywork.

Pickle: a situation about which you or your child has strong feelings.

179

No pickle zone: a place where everything is fun and cool.

Boundaries: behavioral lines that can move.

Rules: behavioral lines that cannot move.

My-messages: messages about me, the speaker. They are messages that I want to convey to you, the listener. They eliminate the negative "you" that blames and accuses.

Opinion: a belief not based on certainty but on what seems to be true or probable.

Problem: a question proposed for a solution.

The Controller: takes charge and makes the other feel impotent.

The Judge: finds fault and makes the other feel stupid.

The Caretaker: praises and agrees making the other's problem feel unimportant.

The Detective: analyzes and makes the other feel defensive.

The Professional Parent: listens for feelings, opens the door for communication, makes the other feel valued and important.

Professional Parent Application

Finishing this workbook and applying the learnings to your family qualifies you as a Professional Parent™.

APPLICATION

(Circle one)

1) Your child comes home with two different art projects.

Do you say...

a)   What a fabulous artist you are!

b)   You're great!

c)   I see lines and colors.

d)   Only two? Where's more?

It's morning, your eight-year-old says, "I'm not going to school today."

Do you say...

a)   So, you don't want to go to school.

b)   Everybody goes to school. Get dressed now!

c)   If you went to bed on time you wouldn't be so tired.

3) Your teenager is going to a party Friday night.

Do you say...

a)   Are there going to be any parents there?

b)   Are there going to be drugs and alcohol?

c)   Curfew is 11:00 pm. Be on time.

d)   I'd like to hear more about what's going on.

4) Your 18-month-old is biting, hitting, and shoving.
Do you...

a)   Leave the area when he starts this behavior.

b)   Say, "No hitting."

c)   Bite him back to show him how it feels.

d)   Remove him from the problem and whisper, "People are not for biting".

5) Your 15-year-old misses the school bus.

Do you...

a) Drive him to school feeling angry and resentful.
b) Tell him it's his problem.
c) Yell at him, and tell him he's irresponsible.
d) Talk to come up with solutions.

6) Your two-year-old is throwing a screaming tantrum in the supermarket.
Do you...

a) Buy him a candy bar to keep him quiet.
b) Yank his arm and tell him to be quiet.

c) Tell him you can't hear what he is saying in his upset voice.

d) Leave the store embarrassed with a screaming child.

7) Does your three-year-old listen to you because...

a) You listen to him.

b) He's frightened.

c) You're angry.

d) He's good.

8) Your two-and-a-half year-old wants to turn on the TV before breakfast.

Do you...

a) Click it off.

b) Give a scowl.

c) Smile and take away the remote.

d) Talk about his feelings.

"We must create for ourselves
new models for adults
who can teach children
not what to learn, but how to learn
and not
what they should be committed to, but
the value of commitment."
Margaret Mead
(1901-1978)

Noted American anthropologist and writer

A License to Parent

Certifies Bearer

Name: _____

Professional Parent

- Looks for feelings behind words
- Evaluates how things are going
- Gets down to eye level
- Has fun, fun, fun

Kaela Austin
Kaela Austin

Cydney Kirschbaum
Cydney Kirschbaum

Kaela & Cydney's Message
To Parents and Children
All Over the World

~~~~~~

Every person who decides that they want to be a parent has the right to have memories of their children that are loving, confronting, learning and positive. Every person who decides to bring children into this world has the right to have wonderful, meaningful relationships with them from the beginning, through adolescence, into their maturing years. Acting on the information in these pages can guarantee, yes guarantee, that kind of relationship between EVERY parent and EVERY child. These are the skills and techniques that we would like people of the world to use so that we can have a universal language, so that we can communicate our differences, express our needs, and at the same time, validate ourselves and others.

Let the good times roll!

How You Can Make A Difference

The "Urban Parent Project" (UPP) is a non-profit organization, directed by the mother/daughter team of Kaela Austin and Cydney Kirschbaum. U.P.P. is a program dedicated to teaching "how to" parenting skills and techniques to the widest number of parents not traditionally targeted for such education. We want to reach everyone, including parents from under-served ethnic and socioeconomic communities. With these parenting techniques, parents can learn to become effective at creating a safer and healthier environment for children by promoting and encouraging self-esteem, self-reliance and self-respect.

Over the past 40 years, theories, strategies, techniques, tactics and tools have been developed by experts to support parents to be more effective. In the early 1960's, Dr. Hiam Ginott pioneered techniques to promote clear and genuine communication between parent and child. The results for participating parents have been extremely gratifying.

UPP's specific focus has been to create programs to educate volunteers in teaching the UPP techniques. This book, "License to Parent" is part of that program. We developed a multilevel approach which includes curriculum materials necessary - workbooks, flash cards, games, etc. - for people to become more successful at parenting.

By educating themselves on how to become more effective at communicating with children, parents can foster an environment of open interaction and integrity where children feel loved, empowered and capable of reaching their potential.

Promoting and encouraging self-esteem, self-respect and self-reliance awakens that potential power in each of us. By teaching and allowing children to identify and express their needs and feelings constructively we can reverse the violent epidemic that is occurring in our schools and in our society.

The "Urban Parent Project" is looking for volunteers to teach our program. We are seeking individuals who are respected members of the community; who want to learn these communication methodologies and take them back to their home areas to teach, and support parents to become more successful at this job of parenting

If you have the desire to make a difference - to make a better and safer place to live and grow, you fit the job description.

To register to become a volunteer trainer, or for more information, please contact: Kaela Austin, Director of the Urban Parent Project:

e-mail: kaela@al2p.com
phone: (310) 390-4229

Business Address:
Urban Parent Project
12228 Venice Boulevard #348
Los Angeles, California 90066